DOCUMENTARY CASE STUDIES

DOCUMENTARY CASE STUDIES

Behind the Scenes of the Greatest (True) Stories Ever Told

JEFF SWIMMER

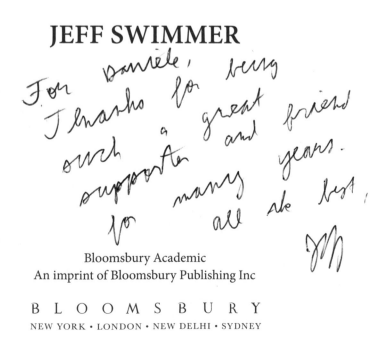

Bloomsbury Academic
An imprint of Bloomsbury Publishing Inc

B L O O M S B U R Y
NEW YORK · LONDON · NEW DELHI · SYDNEY

Bloomsbury Academic

An imprint of Bloomsbury Publishing Inc

1385 Broadway	50 Bedford Square
New York	London
NY 10018	WC1B 3DP
USA	UK

www.bloomsbury.com

BLOOMSBURY and the Diana logo are trademarks of Bloomsbury Publishing Plc

First published 2015

© Jeff Swimmer, 2015

Library of Congress Cataloging-in-Publication Data
Swimmer, Jeff.
Documentary case studies : behind the scenes of
the greatest (true) stories ever told / Jeff Swimmer.
pages cm
Includes bibliographical references and index.
ISBN 978-1-62356-611-1 (hardback : alk. paper) – ISBN 978-1-62356-943-3
(pbk. : alk. paper) 1. Documentary films–History and criticism.
2. Documentary films–Production and direction–History and criticism. I. Title.
PN1995.9.D6S885 2015
070.1'8–dc23
2014029810

ISBN: HB: 978-1-6235-6611-1
PB: 978-1-6235-6943-3
ePub: 978-1-6235-6755-2
ePDF: 978-1-6235-6729-3

Typeset by Integra Software Services Pvt. Ltd.
Printed and bound in the United States of America

For my uncle Marty
loved, and missed, by many

CONTENTS

PREFACE

Writing this book has been an absolute pleasure for me—eye-opening and inspiring in ways I hadn't foreseen. Since 2008, I've taught Documentary Production at Dodge College of Film and Media Arts, at Chapman University. I've noticed over the years how animated students get when they hear behind-the-scenes stories about their favorite films. So, I decided to write a book focused on just those stories.

Documentary filmmaking isn't usually an overly technical affair, and it's certainly not a "flap A fits into flap B..." construction project either. With drive, passion, and some basic storytelling "street smarts," it can be done. I chose the 13 films in these pages to explore a wide range of strategies for meeting production challenges. They range from risky dramatizations, music rights nightmares, prickly subjects, slammed doors at every turn, and the spirit-numbing pain of spending months with serial killers. I hope that the filmmakers sharing their stories can incite others to find fresh and innovative ways to tell their own.

I chose to focus on Oscar-nominated and Oscar-winning films because, whatever one may think of the awards-industrial complex, the films tend to be high profile. Talking to so many filmmakers in the past couple of years, I've noticed some fascinating patterns. First, a huge number of Oscar films are made by first-timers. It drives home that a great idea and tenacity can trump a long track record. It's also a wonderful compliment to the documentary business—barriers to entry are low.

The filmmakers' stories also reminded me anew of the importance of smart partnering. Making documentaries takes months and years, with high stress and low budgets. Partnerships are tested in the extreme, but when they're built on complementary skills—a can't-balance-my-checkbook director with a fundraising whiz, a shooter with an editor, a novice with a veteran—teams can thrive.

The filmmakers also all displayed amazing tenacity. I get chills when I hear filmmakers who simply refuse to let go of a scene, an interview, a moment that seems impossible to capture but which they crave. The best are outrageously resourceful, sometimes deploying a jackhammer, and sometimes a well-phrased whisper, to bust through closed doors.

Personally I've always loved making documentaries because it's the ultimate passport into people, scenes, and situations that would otherwise be closed off. The filmmakers profiled in this book take this concept and run with it in the extreme, leaping over barricades and taking lucky viewers along with them. And the future looks bright for the genre. Clever filmmakers are finding an array of digital homes for their films. I was consistently impressed with how even the oldest documentaries profiled in the book are constantly recycling their work for fresh eyes.

I hope you'll enjoy the ride with them as much as I have.

Jeff Swimmer,
June 2014

ACKNOWLEDGMENTS

Writing can be a lonely endeavor, but I was very blessed to have a team of wonderful people to help buoy me along. First off, I want to warmly thank my colleagues at Chapman University's Dodge College of Film and Media Arts—Dean Bob Bassett, Media Arts Chair Janell Shearer, Associate Dean Michael Kowalski, and my fellow faculty. All of you supported my bid for a sabbatical, which gave me time to bring this book to fruition. And a special appreciation to Chapman University Chancellor Daniele Struppa—thank you for your advice and encouragement.

A very warm thank you to my editor at Bloomsbury, Katie Gallof, who believed in me and the concept for this book, and provided sage counsel and comfort at every step of the way. Thanks also to her Editorial Assistant, Mary Al-Sayed, and to my own Editorial Assistant, Stephanie Lincoln.

To my book agents Eric and Maureen Lasher, with LA Literary Agency, thank you so much. I met you randomly once when I was a wannabe writer in high school, and always hoped to work on a book with you. Decades later, you not only remembered me but believed in me. And I'm most grateful.

I also want to thank my many documentary filmmaking friends and colleagues, who continue to inspire and amaze me with your daring, vision, and tenacity. You give everything to create wondrous works of art, insight, and wisdom in a field where recognition and compensation are so hard to come by. You are my heroes in so many ways.

Lastly, my heroes at home—my family. My magnificent wife and muse Gayle Gilman, and my four children—Ella, Dylan, Colin, and Juliet. You all keep me warm and smiling with your love, humor, wit, and rascally ways. To my always loving parents, Linda and Anson, my wonderful sisters Karen and

Yonat, brothers-in-law, and my many nephews and nieces—thank you for being loving, honest, and encouraging for so many years.

Finally, to my uncle Marty, your love for books and language rubbed off on me, in all the right ways. You are greatly missed.

1

Food, Inc.

DIRECTOR AND PRODUCER
Robert Kenner

PRODUCER
Elise Pearlstein

Oscar Nominee, Best Documentary Feature—2009

SUMMARY

Food, Inc. is a vivid and disturbing examination of America's food supply, finding a system that prioritizes corporate profits above employee and consumer health. A web of cozy government and business ties works to insure that safety for workers and consumers, and corporate fairness, are at the bottom of the food chain.

One day, Robert Kenner set out on a seemingly simple journey—to find out what's on his dinner plate. He quickly discovered it was a secret and one he'd have to move mountains to crack—even slightly.

"The food world," Elise Pearlstein tells me over lunch one day, "is a one-company town." And like one-company towns everywhere, she goes on, the "food-industrial complex" is expert at obfuscation, enforcing lock-step discipline among its inhabitants and intimidating those who dare try to unlock its secrets.

These are undoubtedly wonderful tactics to boost the corporate bottom line, but they're a nightmare for filmmakers like Director Robert Kenner and Producer Elise Pearlstein. So the years they spent making *Food, Inc.* turned into a fascinating and treacherous journey to unveil the mysterious contents of the American refrigerator.

And like so many other rich documentaries, *Food, Inc.* would become a film about way more than its mere subject matter. How our food is made, and by whom, is formally the engine that drives the film, and the universal subject matter and superb quality made it a box office hit. But both Kenner and Pearlstein would come to view food as more of a metaphor for trying to answer much deeper questions. "Food is the sugar coating, but Food, Inc. is really about way more. It's about the right to know … if you live in a free society and you live in a free market you should have the right to information. But it's not free if you don't have that information," says Kenner.

If there was a soundtrack for *Food, Inc.*, it might be the sound of doors slamming in the faces of the filmmakers. At all levels of the food world, from the farmers, distributors, packagers, wholesalers and retailers, nearly all greeted Kenner and Pearlstein with a middle finger raised high in the air. And in hindsight, both came to see they may have been naïve in thinking the experience would prove to be anything else.

Food, Inc.'s story began in 2002, when Kenner read author Eric Schlosser's groundbreaking *Fast Food Nation*, a bravura dissection of the fast-food industry that ripped open its greasy and cynical heart. "I thought *Fast Food Nation* would make a great film, and Eric had seen a film I'd made (*War Letters* for Public Broadcasting Service (PBS) 'American Experience'), and we thought we should make a film together."

Kenner had at that point a sturdy track record making blue-chip documentary films for PBS. His *War Letters* was a deeply moving epistolary account of war as witnessed from the front lines. He was co-filmmaker on "Road to Memphis" for Martin Scorsese's series, *The Blues*, and directed the

Emmy- and Peabody-winning *Two Days in October* (2005) for the American Experience series. He was known as a superb craftsman of ambitious and challenging fare, and set out to secure funding for his latest passion, *Fast Food Nation*. PBS and BBC (British Broadcasting Corporation) signed on to help fund it, and he then went looking for additional funds to help develop it. At the time Participant Productions, as it was then known, was a young company quickly making a name for itself supporting both fiction and non-fiction films with a social message, including the Academy Award-winning *An Inconvenient Truth*. Kenner approached them with the *Fast Food Nation* documentary idea, and they quickly decided to back the project, and then River Road Entertainment joined as a partner.

With Participant's support in place, Kenner brought on Elise Pearlstein as producer. Pearlstein had produced a wide range of innovative non-fiction at that point, having just completed work on director Jessica Yu's avant-garde hit documentary "Protagonist," and a series of hard-hitting segments with veteran newsman Peter Jennings' unit at ABC.

Kenner was now set to make a documentary about *Fast Food Nation*. But during development, his concept of the film began to stretch. "Eric's book was so successful that people thought they could avoid industrialized bad food if they just didn't eat it." In other words, Schlosser's book, alarming as it was, could too easily be written off by consumers: "Fast food may be awful, but it's okay, I don't eat it anyway."

Kenner worried that this let people off the hook too easily. And just as Kenner's team were ruminating over how to broaden the scope of the film, Americans were reeling from an unlikely health scare. In September 2006, a batch of organic spinach contaminated with deadly e-coli virus would end up sickening hundreds and killing three.

Kenner said the e-coli scourge, in supposedly healthy food no less, stiffened his resolve to "broaden out from fast food to the supermarket, because it could affect more people."

Pearlstein concurs. "The spinach outbreak really showed people who think of themselves as enlightened, healthy eaters that they weren't immune from the problems in the food supply," says Pearlstein.

In essence, the filmmakers realized that the industrial supply lines meant that ALL food has become fast food, and that would become the focus of their film.

(*Fast Food Nation* would ultimately become a film but not in its original shape. In 2006, feature director Richard Linklater would turn it into a technically innovative, semi-animated drama.)

Pearlstein and Kenner updated the treatment to reflect its expanded scope and reached out for advice from beloved storyteller and advice-giver on all things food, author Michael Pollan. His mega-selling "The Omnivore's Dilemma" had come out in 2006, and the filmmakers detected a changing mood in America about what people eat. Americans now seemed to want to know what was really in the food on their plate, how it was made, and what it could do to them—healthful or otherwise.

A new kind of national conversation about food was taking shape, and the two wanted the film they were developing to become part of that discussion. With the brilliant and telegenic Eric Schlosser and Michael Pollan helping to guide them along, they set out for the heart of America's food supply.

Kenner had recently finished a documentary where access to subjects and locations was, fortunately for him, relatively easy, and he went into *Food, Inc.* with his fingers crossed. But his reception could hardly have been more different.

"We had a film where people just didn't want to let us in, which was opposite of my last film. People put down walls, even if they were friendly," recalls Kenner. By the time Pearlstein came on board during pre-production, Kenner was already receiving the cold shoulder from many of the food industry's major players. He was getting worried.

But Pearlstein had in recent years come off food industry films where doors had, for various reasons, flung open for her and her team. "I came in really confident, because I had done a documentary with Executive Producer Craig Leake and Peter Jennings that looked at how Frito-Lay was globalizing the potato chip. We had quite full cooperation from Pepsi (Frito-Lay's parent), and they showed us their internal meetings, strategy meetings, inside their factories, and they were really transparent. And the film wasn't a love letter to them. It asked hard questions, but they participated." It was likewise with a film about the Pillsbury Bake-Off Contest that she had done. Its parent, General Mills, cooperated fully.

Kenner appreciated the enthusiasm. "We'll get (the food companies) to talk," she told him. "'I know we will.' Robby was not as optimistic ... and I would say we definitely had unforeseen challenges." And that is probably an understatement. Despite schmoozing, dining and pressing the flesh with food executives who'd cooperated in the past, and those who they hoped would work with them, it was a nearly unanimous "no."

"We essentially heard: 'It's just not in our interest to talk at all'—that was a new development," says Pearlstein. "Even in the few years that had passed from when I had done the other documentaries, there had been kind of a mind-set change, a clamp down on transparency." Pearlstein attributes it to "blame coming at the food industry for soaring rates of obesity, law suits, food outbreaks and fear." In other words, the very factors that ignited their enthusiasm for making the film in the first place were now making it look nearly impossible to make.

Some of the companies agreed to talk but only with promises that the stories would show them in a positive light—obviously, a non-starter.

Years later, Kenner still smarts at some of the close calls they had in terms of access. "I really wanted to film in the International Flavor Factory. It's like Willy Wonka. It's in New Jersey and it's where they create the flavor. I love the woman, and she had loved 'Fast Food Nation' ... she said she only had one concern. 'If I let you in, will I be fired?' And I said, 'that's a very valid concern.' She sent the limo to get me but ultimately was scared."

So thorough was the drumbeat of rejection that Pearlstein was growing worried too. "I was kind of scared … we had a deal to make the film and we knew we had to make the film, but I thought … how are we going to deliver?"

But at a certain point, the rejection parade turned from frustration—to determination. They became even more emboldened to tell the story, no matter who refused to participate. Kenner: "The more we were turned down, the more I realized that these companies are not interested in having consumers see where their food comes from. And the more we were turned down, the more you realized there was something interesting here."

To get footage inside the various farms, factories and slaughterhouses without industry help, they would have to rely on undercover footage. But a 1990s trial involving Food Lion supermarkets put a chill on the *Food, Inc.* team and made that proposition much more difficult. Courts had ruled against ABC News when some of their reporters posed as Food Lion employees and then shot and broadcast clandestine footage. Because of the Red Lion case, "our lawyer told us you can't go in to expose a place if you're not actually already working there and have a valid reason for filming the conditions. If someone has filmed there already, then it's okay." Kenner will not discuss details of how they pulled off getting their secret footage but says it was based on their lawyer's advice: they shot none of it and acquired all of it.

Pearlstein puts it bluntly: "The food industry has a real interest in keeping the process hidden from the public because if the public saw, they wouldn't like what they saw." *Food, Inc.*'s undercover footage is grisly and unsparing—blood-curdling noises coming from slaughterhouses and chicken coops, indifferent fork lift operators trying to force lame downer cattle onto the kill lines, and all manner of animal carcasses being sliced to bits with giant saws and blades. No wonder Variety said *Food Inc.* "does for the supermarket what 'Jaws' did for the beach." Even the bloodless footage—never-ending and spirit-numbing assembly lines of various popular foods being packaged and assembled—leaves a bitter taste in the mouth.

As gory as much of that material is, the filmmakers originally had pushed that even harder. "Participant was good at saying, 'How much do those gory scenes help advance the story?' They were saying, 'a little goes a long way,'" recalls Pearlstein. In the end, Kenner found a happy medium, reminding himself why he wanted to expose the ways of the food industry in the first place: "You don't want to make a film where people have to close their eyes, but you want to make a film where people have to open their minds."

The filmmakers also decided they needed to make industry rejection a part of their film, but they weren't interested in turning the cameras on themselves. So after most of the film's key scenes exposing some kind of industry malfeasance, text on screen appears announcing that Company X refused requests for an interview. After the first few times of using this device, viewers come to expect it. Company snubs become like punctuation marks ending many of the film's chapters—a little going a long way, indeed.

Today, the filmmakers suspect that many of the companies who snubbed them may, with hindsight, even regret the decision. According to Pearlstein, even Monsanto, who comes across in *Food, Inc.* as arch and bullying gene police, may wish they'd participated, as indicated in a Business Week article around the time of the movie's release. A hypothetical *Food, Inc.* sequel, she believes, would field a much stronger corporate line-up. But she's also realistic. "Food companies are in a very difficult position. They know that consumers want more transparency, but I don't think they quite know how to do it."

Food giant Wal-Mart is one of the very few exceptions. They decided to participate. Frequent media punching bags, Wal-Mart comes in for a not unflattering portrayal in the film. Jovial Wal-Mart representatives in modern country garb are seen on the move on a picturesque farm, looking to lock down high volume deals for organic dairy products. Both the characters they meet on-screen and viewers alike have to almost do a double take to reconcile the negative stereotypes of Wal-Mart with the well-meaning and earnest buyers who appear in *Food, Inc.*

Pearlstein explains: "Not that we sugarcoated or tried to make [Wal-Mart] look good, but given the opportunity to actually have a huge corporation in this film we wanted to do right by them and let them make their point well. That's what we always said to people: 'Give us your best spokesperson to make your point.'"

One of the lone industry reps who did agree to present his point-of-view is Richard Lobb, with the National Chicken Council. After showing viewers footage of a typical, vast chicken operation, he speaks plainly to the heart of capitalism: "I try to produce as much as I can for the lowest cost." His parting rhetorical shot lingers in the air, as obvious as it is on point: "Somebody explain to me what's wrong with that?" After the film was released, the Council criticized it for being "one-sided, negative and misleading."

But penetrating giant corporations is challenging no matter the goal or context. What most surprised and frustrated the filmmakers was how far down the food chain, so to speak, the veil of silence was thrown. They were surprised when all of the major food companies refused to go on camera, but what they weren't prepared for was that even the *farmers* refused. "That just did not occur to us," recalls Pearlstein. "Because of the consolidation in the food world, there are only a few companies that really control everything, and all of the farmers are dependent on those companies ... it's a total monopoly land, and if you piss them off, you're out of business."

One chicken farmer who is interviewed, Vince Edwards, typifies the kind of farmer the film sets up as the norm—reluctant to challenge his corporate master, Tyson. Edwards cuts his screen time woefully short. After a candid and sometimes awkward few words, he tells Kenner he can't show them inside any of his operations, implying that there could be consequences from Tyson but careful never to overtly say that. "We'd thought there was a difference between the company and the farmer," confesses Pearlstein.

Chicken farmer Carole Morison, on the other hand, decides that her story needs to be told regardless of the consequences and gives an extensive interview to Kenner and a walking tour through her raucous—but relatively tidy—coops. "Carole was ready to talk, and she and the industry were butting heads so it was a matter of time…I'm not saying she lost her contract because of us but it certainly didn't help." Her contract was technically not renewed because of her refusal to carry out expensive upgrades demanded by the company, but her disgust at her financial plight, and her defiance toward her masters, is vivid. Carole Morison's gritty visage is burned into viewers' minds long after the credits roll.

Pearlstein recalls her experiences with the commercial farmers as especially illuminating. She came to realize that she and Kenner were not only trying to de-mystify the production of food but in essence they were attacking even more fundamental American myths about how we see our relationship to food. "The more you think your food is coming from a little farm with green grass and a beautiful red farmhouse, the more shocking it is to see exactly where it *is* coming from." Ripping the gauzy screen off these core American fantasies would not only shake viewers but also end up transforming the filmmakers as well.

After a financially successful release and the Oscars hoopla, documentary director Kenner would be re-cast as an in-demand, globe-trotting food activist. For years after the release of *Food, Inc.*, he gave talks for at least one week a month, around the world, about the food supply. "Did I want that (outcome?) I didn't contemplate that whatsoever." He's enjoyed being an activist but also missed filmmaking and craved a quick break from heavy social issues. So Kenner took on *When Strangers Click* (2011, HBO), a "vacation film," as he calls it, on a subject about as far from the abattoir as you can get—on-line romance. Since then, he's directed a number of corporate videos and has launched FixFood, a social media-driven, non-profit organization taking on the corporate food industry.

Pearlstein, for her part, found herself personally transformed from the ordeal of making *Food, Inc.* "I became much more rigorous, and I re-committed to the right of free speech. When you see how much people with a lot of power want information suppressed, that definitely gave me the permission to use my rights to show that stuff." Ever since, her producing tactics are much more direct and focused on getting right to the point, with less worry about developing a relationship with sources unless it's needed. *Food, Inc.* shone a sharp light on just how high the stakes were for the food industry. Huge amounts of money at stake means the food world is dangerous territory for curious filmmakers. She still bristles at the memory of discussions with lawyers they'd hired, about what they could say and show—and what they couldn't. She now works as a documentary executive at Participant Media.

The nail-biting started immediately after the film was released. Would the companies depicted try to place a cease and desist order on the film? "We all had many sleepless nights," remembers Pearlstein. In the end, some companies took to the airwaves and filled their websites with critical dissections of the film and its veracity. But, none sued. Kenner and his team attribute this to the rigorous fact-checking they did for every claim made in the film, no matter how insignificant. And since a successful libel suit requires defendants to display not just inaccuracy but "actual malice," they were very scrupulous about not displaying an intent to harm.

For viewers, the overall weight and thoroughness of *Food, Inc.* is dazzling, and even overwhelming at times, but it may be the story of Barbara Kowalcyk that pulls on both the heart and mind in most profound fashion. Kowalcyk is a middle-aged, Republican homemaker from the heartland thrust into being a non-stop activist for food safety after the death of her two-and-a-half-year old son Kevin from e-coli poisoning after eating a hamburger. A handful of lawmakers are seen indulging her pleas for greater scrutiny of food safety, but you can see that David has no chance against Goliath in this legislative duel. Even more heartbreaking is a startling scene toward the end of the film where she is too afraid to answer a question that seems innocuous but is in fact a landmine that almost none of us sees hiding.

Kowalcyk says she cannot, for legal reasons, answer a question about how the ordeal has changed her eating habits. The query, it turns out, is extremely loaded. So-called "veggie libel laws," which have tripped up even the mighty Oprah Winfrey, are simply too daunting to tamper with, even for those literally in mourning from lax food safety laws. "Veggie libel" gives wide scope to the food industry to sue those who dare criticize its products publicly. Viewers can see in Barbara Kowalcyk's discomfort at the question just how deeply the power and threats of the food industry have thrown all of us off balance when it comes to what we eat.

2

Man on Wire

DIRECTOR
James Marsh

PRODUCER
Simon Chinn

Oscar Winner, Best Documentary Feature, 2008

SUMMARY
The behind-the-scenes tale of French wire walker Philippe Petit's dramatic and daring 1974 high wire walk between the twin towers of New York's World Trade Center.

When English documentary producer Simon Chinn first asked around about making a film on high-wire legend Philippe Petit, friends who'd known or worked with Petit begged Chinn to keep a distance—for Chinn's own sake. Amazing story, but a difficult character. Erratic. Stressful. But this only upped the stakes for the dogged producer. Chinn wanted him and would spend about as long pursuing Petit as it would take to make the splendid film that emerged from their encounters. His and director James Marsh's relentless wooing and nurturing of their wary subject birthed the critical and commercial darling, *Man on Wire*.

His quest began in April 2005, when Chinn found himself professionally restless. He was feeling like, in his words, "a corporate gun for hire," working way too hard on a TV drama for a company in financial trouble and feeling a bit adrift. "Ennui was setting in," he recalls. But then one Sunday morning, an idea came to him through the airwaves. He'd overslept and woke up listening on his clock radio to the BBC Radio show "Desert Island Discs," where a "castaway" and guests come on to talk about the music they'd bring with them to a desert island. That day, the castaway was Philippe Petit. His stories about his magic and stunt performances in the streets of Paris as a child, and the way he savored his "artistic crime" of tightrope-walking across the twin towers of the World Trade Center riveted Chinn.

"I was totally and immediately struck by him and his story," says Chinn. By chance, he had lunch the following week with the producer of that show, and he asked her if she thought a documentary would be possible. The reply was blunt: "Don't go near him. He's a control freak." Appetite. Whetted. Then Chinn went and bought Petit's autobiography, *To Reach the Clouds*, and his zeal to make the film grew even more. There was no suppressing his ardor: "He was just an extraordinary man." So, Chinn reached out to Petit directly about making a film, and got an answer that didn't surprise him at all: "Join the queue…"

The non answer didn't come from Petit but from his chief gatekeeper and partner in all things, Kathy O'Donnell. "Philippe doesn't use email, he doesn't have a mobile phone, nothing like that. Kathy protects him from the world so he can go be this creative force," explains Chinn. She made it clear to Chinn that there were several others who'd already inquired about making a film on Petit's life and work. But Chinn stayed in touch with O'Donnell and found out that Petit would be coming to England to work on a stage adaptation of his memoir.

O'Donnell invited Chinn to meet Petit there in person. But that first meeting was a disaster. "I wasn't prepared, I got stuck in traffic, and I was terribly late. I made the worst impression. I was so disappointed and angry with myself," Chinn recalls, ruefully. But instead of discouraging him, he says the awful encounter "tripled my resolve."

Blunted by an underwhelmed and skeptical Petit, Chinn licked his wounds and turned back to wooing O'Donnell. "I realized I really needed to impress her," he said, and as time wore on, he sensed that his campaign was slowly starting to bring him back into the duo's good graces. She started dropping welcome clues, hinting that other Petit film suitors might not be experienced enough. She urged Chinn to write Petit a creative proposal for a collaboration, in the form of a formal letter. So Chinn lavished over the document, spelling out the exact nature of a partnership, a production schedule, and other details on his wish list.

Finally, Petit called him. Chinn was nervous. Petit told him that, yes, he could shoot him, but not a film about his life—just to promote a tightrope walk he planned over the Grand Canyon. Chinn was furious at Petit's agreeing to something so small but not to the quarry he was really after. Chinn got irate with him even though he knew anger could wreck his chances of making any sort of film about the Frenchman. It was a tactical risk, but Chinn was at his wits' end. "Would he admire me more for tenacity than diplomacy?" he wondered. As it turned out, yes, he did. Petit seemed to admire Chinn's passion and spunk. If it was a test, Chinn might have passed, and his hopes were suddenly alive again.

A summit with the two followed, in Paris. A determined Chinn prepped like crazy for the gathering and made sure to turn up precisely on time. He even played a trick of his own. After finding out, by chance, that Petit was an obsessive color-coder, Chinn very carefully color coded his research notes. During dinner, he nonchalantly started leafing through the notes and Petti's eyes lit up: "You're a color coder like me!" And at that point, Chinn says he just knew in his bones: "I got him. He's mine." Petit handed Chinn a coffee table edition of his book inscribed with the words Chinn had craved for months: "Let's do it."

But as with most things Petit, it would not be easy. After embracing his new partner in Paris, the supremely confident showman made Chinn walk across a series of legal tightropes for another six months of tense, volatile negotiations about the terms of their agreement. Chinn and his lawyers haggled tenaciously over the rights to the book and terms. At one point, in a marathon phone call, Petit and O'Donnell's lawyer ended up screaming at Chinn's production team and their lawyers. But in the end, peace was struck, and Chinn ended up with the element that they prized above all: Petit would have consultative rights on the production but not any contractual rights to approving any content. "All that did was give us the obligation to listen to him, but by God, was he going to be heard!" recalls Chinn. And, in truth, legalistics aside, each needed the other to pull it off. Chinn would need Petit's cooperation all throughout the production and then marketing the film. If Petit turned against the film team, Chinn knew, he could upend the whole enterprise.

Perhaps banged up a bit, but intent on executing their newly struck deal, the two sides then worked to find a director that Petit could accept. He had veto power over the director, and Chinn knew very well he'd likely exercise that right liberally.

Chinn had been developing the film, and negotiating with Petit and his team, from a very attractive home base. His company, Red Box Films, partnered on the project with the prestigious Wall To Wall, one of the United Kingdom's leading production companies. An executive there suggested to him that he ask the director James Marsh to take on the Petit project. Marsh had directed documentaries for some of the BBC's most celebrated and innovative series, and he'd also made the experimental, darkly comic and cultishly popular "Wisconsin Death Trip" (1999).

Marsh, for his part, couldn't have been more grateful for a chance at the high-profile film this could become. For in that summer of 2006, Marsh was in the dumps—on many fronts. He'd just come off an unhappy experience in the narrative filmmaking world. He'd made a feature called "The King," which tanked at the box office and garnered mostly sour reviews. He'd not done a documentary in three years, and was feeling "sort of washed up at that point." He was so broke that he had to send his wife back to her native Denmark with his kids for the summer, while he sublet their Brooklyn apartment and Marsh slept on the floor at a friend's house. In this precarious state of affairs, Marsh threw himself headlong into the treatment, script, outline, and timetable for *Man on Wire*.

Chinn strongly backed Marsh, known for his efficiency, production rigor and a ballooning imaginative style, feeling that he was a strong storytelling choice and a fitting match for the film's demanding subject.

With the key members of the production team in place, the film locked down funding from the BBC, the UK Film Council, and Discovery Films (part of Discovery Channel) in the United States. Each came in with about a third of the total 1.2 million pound budget.

Now they needed to get Petit to agree to their director.

But Marsh's first phone conversation with Petit, as with Chinn, did not go well. "Initially, he wasn't very impressed with Simon and he wasn't very impressed with me. He's quite a difficult man when you first encounter him … He wasn't going to work with somebody he didn't want to work with, and so that was a great, tricky dance," recalls Marsh. Marsh realized he would have to launch the kind of courtship with Petit that his producer partner had just endured.

And so, as with Chinn, Marsh soldiered on and suggested they meet in person, hoping this might go better than the unhappy phone call. "After a long, alcoholic lunch, he told me as we left, 'Let's do this together. I want to do this with you.'" Marsh thought he was home free, but then realized that what he thought was the final exam, was really more of a pop quiz. "That was just one of several early tests he set for me … "

Critically, after getting the thumbs-up from Petit, Marsh would still have to wait for six months before Petit would get to him the archives of his life and work. Petit made clear to Marsh that he saw himself not merely as the subject of the film but also as a collaborator—a dicey situation for any filmmaker. "That can be a very dangerous thing for a filmmaker and his subject, because they are not always the best judge of their own stories," Marsh says. "The production could be quite combative, built on a kind of affection we had for each other as people."

That tough love way of interacting could involve near fisticuffs one minute and embracing the next. This would last for much of the production. After their bumpy first steps, Marsh says he often had to swat away many of Petit's shoot plans. "His ideas for the film were often either impossible to execute or self-defeating," Marsh insists. That said, Petit's ideas couldn't be hastily dismissed because his cooperation was vital. Near constant give-and-take, and testy negotiating over points large and small followed the headstrong men to the finish line. It may have gotten "sparky," recalls Marsh, "but never ugly or personal."

"You have to have strong opinions in filmmaking," says Marsh. "If you don't you shouldn't be making films. So definitely we clashed as we were making the film, but never in a way that was personal. It was always about the ideas. And we always still liked each other even when we fell out or had disputes about the subject matter and who to interview."

Marsh recalls, for example, how Petit was adamant that they not interview two of Petit's key American co-conspirators. Petit felt they didn't carry their weight in the operation and wouldn't fit into the heroic portrayal of the wire walk that he was hoping for. Marsh partly agreed with Petit's assessment: "They were feckless in some respects. They were not reliable." But Marsh wasn't about to toss away two characters who may have been bumblers but indeed were among a very small group of people in the thick of the action during the wire walk. "There was no question to interview them whether he liked it or not. And he didn't like it. But to give him credit, he saw the value of them when the film was finished."

Petit also wanted to be on set for key interviews as often as he could, even for scenes where he was not directly needed. The filmmakers saw this as a major distraction. "He wouldn't accept being forbidden from the set, but I talked him out of it. I persuaded him that it would not be a good idea," says Marsh. Marsh felt Petit, with his big personality and vocal opinions, would have been too risky to have around during key scenes. He was prepared to insist Petit leave if things got dicey, but luckily for both, it never came to that. In the end, Marsh's simple but stern requests did the trick.

Marsh attributes the tense but relatively peaceful mood that prevailed over the course of the year of production in large part to the amount of time the two spent off camera. Marsh wanted badly that Petit not simply see the filmmakers as "extracting" material for a final goal. Many hours—off-set—of listening to music, cracking jokes, eating and drinking, all helped buoy the mood for what might otherwise been a much more difficult arrangement. "That was what he wanted, and that's what I wanted too. He's labor intensive, but I enjoyed his company too. So this trust developed across time," says Marsh.

But despite the frequent drumbeat of tension with his subject, making the film was an exhilarating joyride for James Marsh, a perfect format for him to make use of a whole directorial "bag of tricks" he'd always wanted to deploy together in a film. "I see the film as sort of a sum expression of all the things I knew and liked about the medium itself … It was a chance to make something great for the big screen." Even this quintessentially "glass is half empty" Brit will go out (very far!) on a limb to admit of *Man on Wire* that "this one I quite liked."

The film has a powerful way of never trying too hard to win viewers' attention and yet does so with ease at nearly every turn. The story is delivered with confidence and a hypnotic style, as viewers are lured as accomplices into the dazzling crime to which the story builds. Even though viewers know the outcome of Petit's wire walk, the film still manages to capture genuine drama, a feeling of high stakes, and dense emotional freight wrapped around the culminating stunt. Even three decades later, the filmmakers capture Petit and his wire walk partners with frequent tears in their eyes and looking up in the air, expectantly, as they describe the events of August 9, 1974.

A key breakthrough, in terms of their approach to the material, was when Marsh and Chinn decided that the film needed to be told as a genre film—as a heist story, with the heist in the foreground and then weaving in the past to give the caper shape and context. They had laid out the story chronologically but felt it lacked excitement. "Philippe wrote his memoir as a sort of caper, where half the struggle wasn't the walking on the wire—that was the sort of easy part. It was the actual adventure of getting in. This appealed to him as sort of a mischief-making petty criminal, and to me too," Chinn says.

Drawing our attention to the build-up to the wire walk—rather than the walk itself—serves two purposes. On the one hand, it's a riveting escapade—tricking all the security guards, getting up to the not-quite-finished Twin Towers, setting the cables for the walk, etc. These plot points allow Marsh to lay on thick helpings of the heist genre motifs and look—lean black-and-white dramatizations, taut and minimalist music, plenty of visual play with darkness and shadows. And by making the build up to the stunt the film's narrative engine, viewers are drawn away from the moot "Will he or won't he make it across?" questions.

Add to this a strange twist in the tale that no one could have foreseen. Petit's point person for the arduous job of rigging the massive cables across the Twin Towers that day was his key ally, Jean-Louis Blondeau. But on the morning of the walk, a series of slip-ups made that already difficult job even more physically taxing for Blondeau. To make things worse, rigging cables was not his only job that morning. He was also the designated cameraman. He had a 16 mm film camera with him, but was so drained from hauling cables that he could not even lift the camera—let alone shoot with it.

So the filmmakers would have to make do with a small and motley batch of mostly out-of-focus stills Petit's team shot, to capture the climatic moment of the whole film. To Marsh, this was the biggest production challenge they faced. Animation? Special effects? Might not look credible, or fit with the rest of the film's tone. Then Marsh began mulling over one of his favorite films, the grand and mournful *La Jetee* (1962) made by Chris Marker using almost exclusively still photos. "Chris Marker is a genius. I'm not. But if Chris Marker can do a whole time travel, apocalyptic story with just found photographs, then I should be able to somehow render this walk with actual photographs of the walk. We just had to trust these above all else." And so they did. No effects of any kind. A sequence of slow moves, and the film's insistent, haunting score, would carry these scenes through very capably. Also, the team relied on frequent cutaways to the enraptured recollections of the team there that day. In particular, his girlfriend at the time, and Blondeau, give intensely moving and emotional insights, looking heavenward as they recall the frightful and luminous moments when Petit seemed to float in the sky. "They put us up on that wire, very successfully," says Marsh.

Marsh and Chinn would take another major narrative risk to tell the tale of a seminal event that went largely undocumented by either still images or film. They chose to rely heavily on dramatizations, using actors to play Petit and his wide cast of co-conspirators, antagonists and lovers. Marsh had done dramatizations before for BBC documentaries, and was keen to take on the technique for the big screen. The whole film is structured along parallel paths—one being the action in the days before and including the walk, and the other, longer view, about how they all got to that point in the first place. Both broad paths, woefully lacking in archival material, would require heavy use of dramatization to work effectively.

But any dramatizing in documentaries is problematic. The technique has a controversial reputation, and it's one that has divided many broadcasters and filmmakers for years. Some embrace it as a cost-effective way to add energy to scenes for which there is no visual record, and as a device that affords a high-degree of control in terms of look and pacing. Many others, though, abhor it, calling it visually cheesy and claiming it forces filmmakers to take sides and editorialize when they recreate scenes for which they have little detailed knowledge. The *Man on Wire* team was acutely aware of this debate. "You have to be very wary," says Marsh. "You're bending the form … you're representing your own imagery against people's stories in a way that's entirely invented." Chinn too adds that it always a roll-of-the-dice. "You do them, I guess, more out of necessity than out of design. You just hope you're going to be ambitious, and the reenactments will have, at the very least, some real production value."

So to combat some of the built-in problems with dramatization, Marsh and Chinn took a number of steps to try to use them most effectively. They worked to get copious details about actions and locations from those whom they were preparing to dramatize, they mixed dramatizations with still photos whenever they felt those could boost veracity, and they made the decision to never use any sync dialogue with the dramatizations. Dialogue, they decided, would be pushing an already risky technique one step too far.

Marsh scripted the dramatizations as precisely as he could, and the team took 5 very long days to shoot them after most other filming was complete. They are directed simply, typically with very few characters in frame and scant camera movement. In sync with the fairy tale, Peter Pan-like atmosphere conjured up by Petit, the direction is fanciful and relaxed, rather than obsessed with exact replication. The black-and-white scenes carry us through many of the plot points leading to the wire walk, and it's hard to see how else they could have proceeded. Reaching for us as much verisimilitude as they could gather, the team even persuaded the owners of the building that is replacing the destroyed World Trade Center to let them film from the top of the not yet completed structure, providing them a very similar vantage point to that Petit saw from the towers in August 1974.

As with so much of the shooting for *Man on Wire*, the filmmakers had to wrestle with Petit's wishes when shooting the dramatizations too. Even though everyone they filmed in the dramatizations was an actor, Petit wanted to play himself. The answer? A firm no. Not helpful.

Petit also wanted to do part of his interview going up a tree on a cherry picker, for sentimental reasons—he used to climb trees as a child. The filmmakers broke open their wallets and had a cherry picker drive up from Manhattan to Petit's farm upstate. The interview, however, didn't come off well, and it never made it into the film.

But the filmmakers did find an imaginative way to accommodate one of Petit's requests, and it ended up paying off enormously. Petit, the consummate showman, asked the team: "How about if I perform my interview, re-enact it?" Marsh was open to it, but wasn't sure where this was headed. The producer, Simon Chinn, worried the format would invite Petit to veer off course, to embellish or would simply look too weird. But, they went along with Petit's idea of a "dramatized interview," and the fruits of these odd and inspired scenes end up being some of the most memorable in the whole film.

"It ended up being a wonderful idea because it freed Philippe to be who he really is. He's a performer, and he performed his interview. It was, to a large extent his own mythologizing of his own story. But you know what? It works," admits Chinn.

At one point during this interview, describing how he and his team had to hide from security guards under blankets in the building's upper reaches, Petit drapes a blue cloth over his head and whispers the tale. There's a wonderfully mischievous and childlike quality to the recounting, like a young boy in a tree fort passing along a secret code to his clubmates. At another point, Petit demos how they strung cables between the towers using colored string slung across a scale model of the towers—another delightful and whimsical touch.

"This is an unusual gift, to have your principal contributor, who is a showman, who wants to enact his story. By doing this he was connecting with the emotions that he experienced at the time," says Marsh.

Petit's re-enacted interview bites are woven in with more conventional bites, and viewers enjoy a rounded sense of the film's star, both "on" and "off" stage, as it were. Marsh and his team worked at a fairly quick clip, shooting while cutting, and after a year or so of on-off shooting, by Fall of 2007 the bones of the vérité and archival material are edited. Instead of ending on the triumph of the wire walk, though, Marsh makes the decision to play up the bitter feelings between Petit and his co-conspirators that erupted almost immediately after he got off the wire, and which have mostly lasted to this day. "It's like, they were all up in the air together. He comes down, and everything is different. It's bittersweet. But it's real life—not a superhero movie," says Marsh.

In the early going, there had also been a brief discussion about whether or not, or how, to mention the grisly fate of Petit's towers on September 11, 2001. No way, insisted the filmmakers. "I made the film, in my own mind, to rebuild the Towers," says Marsh. To him, the culminating act of the Towers was Petit's majestic walk, not the vicious attacks that felled them 27 years later. "This film could, its own very small way, give you an hour and a half with the buildings as if they were alive in the best possible life they had. Not the business of American capitalism that went on there, but this beautiful performance."

In the fall of 2007, the team submitted *Man on Wire* to Sundance, and got accepted into the World Documentary competition. Sundance slotted its premiere in the perhaps not-so-glamorous second week of the festival. During the screening, the vibe seemed to be going well when the filmmakers were baffled by a small exodus of people suddenly leaving the theater. But as it turned out, it wasn't their film that provoked the departures. Hollywood star Heath Ledger had just died in New York, word was filtering down to Utah, and some attendees stepped out to swap news about the death. Despite little pre-screening publicity, buzz about *Man on Wire* built quickly after it screened, and it would end up winning a rare double coup—both the Grand Jury Prize and the Audience Award.

Soon after Sundance, Magnolia Pictures struck a deal to release it theatrically, box off receipts came in strong, and then the capper—an Oscar nomination for Best Documentary Feature of 2008. And the following Spring, it won that Oscar. And even Philippe Petit, who claimed to dislike the movie when it was finished, seemed to warm to it as audiences did too. "I think he wouldn't have made it that way himself, but he did end up respecting what we'd done with his story," Marsh says, reflecting on Petit's reaction. And perhaps, the director speculates, "we gave him a whole other sort of cool all over again."

3

Super Size Me

DIRECTOR AND PRODUCER
Morgan Spurlock

Oscar Nominee, Best Documentary Feature—2004

SUMMARY
Morgan Spurlock's gross-out gastronomic journey delivers plenty of shock and humor, while fundamentally probing serious questions: What are our fast food habits doing to our bodies, and to our society?

Super Size Me is a raucous, low-fi, high-impact rant aimed at America's self-destructive obsession with fast food. We watch slender Morgan Spurlock balloon into the oblong shapes of the obese American Everyman, cringing as he pummels his heart, lungs, liver, and brain with a McDonald's-only diet for 30 days.

The affable host takes viewers deep into his body's rapid decline, including into orifices we might prefer to keep a distance from. But he's so likable, easygoing and engaging even as he free falls into near total liver failure and psychic collapse that we can't turn away from his mad experiment.

Criticized by some purists as a shock film, or stunt, the movie ended up forcing Americans to take a much deeper look at their rampant food lust.

"I've been stopped in airports where people pull pictures out of their wallets and say, 'this is me 150 pounds ago. Your film was really a wake up call,'" Spurlock notes, still seeming a little blown away by it all. His monumental feat of near immolation got stunning payback when McDonald's did away with its Super Size option just 6 weeks after the film was released; Spurlock earned back vast sums for his $50,000 roll-of-the-dice movie; and the film launched a cottage industry in cameras-rolling 30 Day-style stunt programming.

Seed money for *Super Size Me* came from the proceeds of another stunt-style show Spurlock and a group of friends had just completed, MTV's "I Bet You Will." "We would go out and get people to do silly things for money on the street," he says. Spurlock stretched this slight concept from the Internet to 53 episodes on MTV before an abrupt cancellation and banked about $50K for his efforts.

He found himself, in 2002, recovering on the couch after an especially overindulgent Thanksgiving dinner with his family. Overeating was on his mind as he was foraging for a good subject for his next project. Flipping through news channels, he was struck by the now notorious story of two grossly overweight New York teenagers who sued McDonald's, claiming the company caused their obesity.

"They basically said: 'We're fat. We're sick. And it's your fault.' And I said, well, that's crazy!"

When McDonald's came back and said its food was in fact nutritious, Spurlock was just as blown away as he was with the girls' claims.

"I was, like, well, 'if it's that good for me, shouldn't I be able to eat it for 30 days with no side effects?' And then, boom, at that moment, the light went on and I was, like, 'oh my god, I've got a great idea for a movie.'" But the feeling was hardly unanimous.

His vegan girlfriend gave him a big thumbs down to the idea, calling it "probably the worst idea ever." Check. His sales agent, John Sloss, said: "I don't know who would want to see that." So far so good. Then he shared his plan with his working partner, cinematographer Scott Ambrozy. After a long silence, he got back exactly the response he was hoping for: "Wow, that's a really great bad idea." Taking that as a green light, their next challenge was finding a "guinea pig" to undergo the wretched ordeal.

Michael Moore's in-your-face, smash hit *Bowling for Columbine* (2002) had just come out and sparked excitement about the possibilities for the hosted documentary format. Spurlock loved the "guided tour" style Moore had had such success with and looked for someone who could pull off the same with his digestive journey concept.

But casting proved problematic. "How will we know if we stop shooting for the day and the host isn't cheating, going home and sneaking some broccoli or some bok choi?"

Spurlock, a gregarious West Virginian with a brief background in standup comedy, realized he had no choice but to quit casting and to put himself to the test, cameras rolling. Spurlock was very health conscious and recalls growing up eating raw vegetables from his backyard as a small boy. "We only ate junk food in our house when my mom was sick, or angry." But now he'd have to turn his back on all that and head in the opposite direction. His hosting seems like a foregone conclusion today, but it was an agonizing decision at the time. "It's frightening. It's scary to put yourself in that position. You do open yourself up to a tremendous amount of exposure that you may or may not want, that you may or may not be able to stomach."

So, just a few weeks after the light bulb went off in his head during his family's Thanksgiving bacchanal, everything was in place for him and his team to begin the grisly assault on his body.

No more excuses, no alibis. "We had the MTV money, so we didn't have to wait to find financing. We owned all the equipment [from the MTV show], and my DP [Director of Photography] moved in and started shooting. It was a perfect storm," Spurlock recalls. Spurlock knew all too well the pitfalls of production delay and was obsessed with keeping up momentum.

But spending his MTV "windfall" on a film was a massive risk, because Spurlock was massively in debt. "I was paying my rent with credit cards. I was paying my employees with credit cards. I was paying *their* rent with credit cards. I was even paying credit cards with credit cards!" He'd been evicted from his apartment in New York when he couldn't come up with rent and was living in a hammock in his office. More sensible souls would have used those 50,000 dollars to plug holes in his hemorrhaging debt. But Spurlock decided on a huge roll of the dice.

Shooting would begin February 1, 2003, and would end exactly 30 days later, March 2.

But as production drew closer, Spurlock began to have doubts about throwing all his darts at one single fast food chain. When there were so many similar "villains," why go after just one? Was his target off base? Filmmaker friends told him it was too narrowly focused. "Go after the other chains too!" was a frequent refrain. He considered casting a wider net but ultimately came back to his first instinct: "McDonald's is such a sacred cow in our society. … It's just the biggest of them all. If there was an effort to affect change here, it just had to come from the top."

But by choosing to take on such a Goliath, Spurlock knew he was opening himself up to legal threats from McDonalds' army of lawyers. With creditors circling, he was planning not only to spend his entire nest egg, but he would be exposing himself to massive legal bills as well, which could easily ruin him. His $50,000 might just last for a one-month shoot and a quick Post-Production, but he'd have not a penny to spare to defend himself in court. So he read everything he could about documentaries and libel and also called in favors with every lawyer he could think of to try to put together a legal team. To his surprise, he managed to cobble one together—entirely pro bono. Even so, he recalls, nightmares about McDonald's lawyers kept him up at night for years. "We kept thinking, wow, they are really going to come after us, aren't they?"

To try to stretch out their budget, they made some key production decisions—no one gets paid unless the movie recoups, no equipment rentals and no frills of any kind. On February 1, shooting begins, and the crew is as bare bones as can be—just Spurlock and his DP, Scott Ambrozy. "I was booking all the interviews. Scott was dealing with all the shooting and the lights, and he and I were putting the microphone on somebody and doing the audio." Small camera, boom mic, lavalieres, tripod, and that's it.

They also decided that, for practical reasons, it was important not to over-reach. Dream big but be realistic and lower expectations at every turn. "A friend of mine is a photographer, and I once asked him, 'What's your favorite camera?' He said, 'It's the one in my hand.' You do the best with what you have." That sober, blunt logic would have to guide their shoot, even though, financially, the stakes couldn't be higher. Spurlock was throwing money into an outrageously risky venture, and financial and legal worries hung over the duo every day of the shoot. And for Spurlock, it was far worse, as he had to continue to direct all the action and make creative decisions even as he slaughtered his body and mind with toxins.

When they set out, neither he nor any of the doctors who monitored Spurlock had any idea how severely and quickly his body would decline while on the diet. But they decided right away that, whatever happened, they wouldn't hold anything back. "There'd be nothing too raw or disgusting for this movie. From me having an (on-camera) rectal exam, throwing up out of a car window, and my girlfriend talking about our sex life ... It's just freak show enough to get people engaged, but not gross enough where it will turn people off."

And unsparing it is. The scene early on where he sits in a car and throws up a massive meal, with barely enough time to roll down the window, would became a fan favorite. But the question hung over them constantly—"How far do we push things?" For most of the film, Spurlock appears a bloated, woozy and depressive mess. Near the end of the film, tests reveal that he has so wrecked his body, viewers might begin to worry they're about to watch a snuff film. Doctors beg him to stop but he foolishly presses on, without giving any convincing reasons why. The film is self-abusive in the extreme. "Somebody said this was like 'Jackass' journalism, and that's exactly what it is. We've used this stunt, and my body, to study what's happening in a way that makes it accessible to a lot of different people."

Unflattering as it was, from a production standpoint the project had some key advantages. The "30-day" hook, which Spurlock improvised, imposed a strict shooting discipline on the duo and gave them a clear end point for shooting that so many documentary filmmakers struggle to find. "When do I stop shooting?" bedevils countless filmmakers, but Spurlock had a built-in deadline. "You know that literally in five weeks, you'll be done shooting. When you're out in the field and you see something and you miss it, you have to say, great, and move on. You can't harbor anything. The minute something's done, you move on." That ruthless logic saved them both time and money and created a hyper-fast template that Spurlock would impose on more of his films in the future.

Spurlock took another valuable lesson from the pell-mell *Super Size Me* pace. While he and his team broke speed records on the shoot, he kicks himself for starting the edit too late—in June, a few months after shooting. They lost some momentum and saw story flaws only when it was too late. Spurlock vowed never to make the same mistake again and promised to edit all future films at the same time as shooting. "That way we can already see the story developing, holes that we need to fill, pieces that are missing in our narrative. I wish we'd started editing (*Super Size Me*) earlier for those very reasons." Of course *Super Size Me* was an unusual case, because the making of it nearly killed the filmmaker. After the 30 days, Spurlock was some 25 pounds heavier and wrecked inside and out—hardly the best state for an edit. His girlfriend put him on an intensive, de-tox diet to clean out and get him ready for the cut.

Spurlock also wanted editors with strong opinions, who wouldn't back off from picking a fight over material. No button-pushers. At one point in Post, Spurlock was looking to cut for time and suggested losing the scenes about the copious amount of junk foods being served in school cafeterias. "Are you kidding? No way will we cut that out," the editors told him. "Those scenes show how deeply we've infiltrated our kids and culture with this stuff." In the end, the editors made the right call. The school lunch scenes are teeth-gritting ordeals, where stammering cafeteria workers and students alike try to justify the grotesqueries in the chow line.

While cutting, he sought out a documentary filmmaker whose work he admired—Eugene Jarecki. "He said, 'If the movie you end up with is the exact same movie you envisioned in the beginning, then you didn't listen to anybody along the way.'" Spurlock said that advice kept him getting locked into tunnel vision about the story line. "There's always going to be somebody who opens three doors that you never thought were possible, and you have to afford yourself the ability to go through those doors. That was the greatest advice I ever got, and could ever give."

They sent the film to Sundance, and got in, but expectations were low. Their sales agent thought a cable deal or DVD were a possibility and that's about it. To Spurlock's surprise, when he showed up to the first screening, all the biggest buyers and distributors were there—MGM, Fox, Paramount and many others. Their reaction was uniform: "We loved the film, but one by one they admitted they just couldn't do it, because they realized they needed those partners, those toys and Happy Meals, and these very valuable marketing partnerships."

One distributor, though, was willing to take a chance on it: Samuel Goldwyn. Spurlock says the only reason they took that risk was because of the work of another filmmaker: "Michael Moore's *Roger and Me* and *Bowling for Columbine* paved the way, saying as long as you dot your i's and cross your t's, you can make a film that will generate a tremendous amount of word of mouth and buzz, but at the same time hold up to any sort of legal questions."

And in the end, to his and his team's astonishment, McDonald's never did send any lawyers after them. Toward the end of *Super Size Me*, Spurlock is seen calling repeatedly to try to arrange an interview with someone, anyone, from McDonald's. They refused. Spurlock attributes the distance the company kept from his film in the years after it was released to a simple decision—they hoped the film would quietly go away, and they wanted to avoid giving it any more publicity. They probably didn't want to turn Spurlock into an underdog in a way that would burnish Spurlock's guerrilla cred even more.

McDonald's kept Spurlock at arm's length. "When I would go on a TV show, they would never come on simultaneously, but just before me or after me … they would never want to come on and have a real debate with me about the issue. They played it off like I was just some lunatic. And what I continued to bring up with them is, sure, what I'm doing is pretty extreme, but what you see happening to my body over 30 days is what you see happening to a person's body over a lifetime of eating this food. High blood pressure, heart disease, liver failure … "

Lucky timing also favored the *Super Size Me* team. McDonald's had, just prior to the film's release, lost a very high-profile case in the United Kingdom that probably made them a little bit gun shy by the time *Super Size Me* came out. The case would become known as the "McLibel trial," and lasted longer than any trial in British history. Two low-key Brits—one a postman and the other a gardener, named Dave Morris and Helen Steel respectively, handed out leaflets to the public in the 1980s attacking McDonald's for promoting dangerous eating habits, exploiting children, and harming the environment. McDonald's took them to court, accusing them of libel. But in the late 1990s, first a British judge and then a European Union judge delivered a series of devastating rulings in favor of Morris and Steel, lacerating McDonald's corporate image in sharply worded rulings.

So by 2003, Spurlock and his team calculated that McDonald's may have still been licking their McLibel wounds and might not have the stomach for another fight. "If it had not been for the McLibel Trial, McDonald's would have definitely come after me. I think when they went through binders of mistakes they made in the past, they said, 'Let's treat this one very differently.' And in the United States, they pretty much ignored us." But it was not the case overseas.

McDonald's launched a massive campaign against the film in places with more relaxed libel laws, like Australia, where the CEO of McDonald's Australia appeared on screen just before the film to denounce it as a lie. In the United Kingdom, the company took out full-page ads in all of the major newspapers attacking the film for spreading lies. To Spurlock, all that money Mcdonald's spent overseas simply ended up lining his own pocket. "It was spectacular. They gave me the greatest marketing campaign for this movie outside of America that I could have ever hoped for."

When the movie finally did hit the theaters, Spurlock was biting his nails. Theaters had been ruthless to documentaries for years, spitting out countless terrific films after brutally short runs and yielding box office receipts that Hollywood's worst bombs would have sneered at. Spurlock feared the worst. "But a friend of mine was in Dallas, Texas the weekend we opened, and there were three movies playing in the theater—*Van Helsing*, *Troy*, and *Super Size Me*. So I asked my friend, 'Is my theater completely empty?' And he says, 'No, it's packed—completely sold out.' I said, that's crazy." Box office statistics were showing that the film was even being embraced by a high percentage of young people, a rarity for any documentary. For many, it was the first documentary they'd ever seen.

After profits started to come in, Spurlock was able to pay the partners who'd helped him make it for deferred salaries. Spurlock took his 30-Day format to great success on TV and created several other successful documentaries after that, including *Where in the World Is Osama Bin Laden* (2008), *The Greatest Movie Ever Sold* (2011), and the massive budget 3-D theatrical hit, *One Direction: This Is Us* (2013) about the English boy band.

A pound of flesh, indeed.

4

Twenty Feet from Stardom

DIRECTOR AND PRODUCER
Morgan Neville

Oscar Winner, Best Documentary Feature—2013

SUMMARY
The fascinating lives of backup singers, who have played pivotal roles in popular music for decades, but who find it tough to catch a break outside the large shadows cast by the singers and bands they support.

"It's a long walk … it's a long walk," intones Bruce Springsteen, a fitting mantra by way of welcome into *Twenty Feet from Stardom*, Morgan Neville's hit documentary about the lives of pop music backup singers. A long haul indeed, as we discover when we meet the high-octane cast of just-off-center-stage divas and dreamers who populate Neville's enormously likable film.

Those backup singers bold enough to aim for the lead singer's microphone inevitably hit brick walls. Sometimes those walls are self-made, and other times they're built by a music industry bent on strict hierarchy, on both stage and in studio.

Twenty Feet's huge success has vaulted the careers of not only its creators but its subjects as well. "I chose the women for the film because I really feel they are uniquely talented and brilliant, and I wanted other people to share in that. And all of them have had a career resurgence because of the film," Neville says with pride. A Rose Bowl halftime appearance, couch time with the likes of David Letterman and Jay Leno, and a media storm have lifted all ships involved with *Twenty Feet*.

For Neville, the film's birth was serendipitous, like a gift-wrapped winning lottery ticket for the veteran music documentary director. "I love music, I'm a music geek through and through, and I think it's a great way to tell stories," says Neville. "This project came about in a way I've never had a project come about before."

Neville got the phone call that led to *Twenty Feet* in early 2011. By then, he'd spent years producing and directing docs on a variety of topics for the big screen and television but with a special love for documentaries about music. He was a reliable go-to guy for the genre not just because of an extensive track record, contacts and directing chops but also because he had the stomach for the notoriously unappetizing work of securing music rights. Dealing with performers, estates, lawyers, record labels, and the *jambalaya* of music rights holders present a scary mine field for many documentary filmmakers. It's nerve-wracking, time-consuming and expensive work, but Neville made a name for himself as one in the business who didn't flinch at rights madness.

Neville was approached by music industry veteran Gil Friesen, who had co-founded A&M Records ("Gil was the ampersand in A&M" is the running joke.) Friesen told him a story, which led to a lightbulb going off on his head, which would eventually lead to *Twenty Feet*. Friesen had recently gone to see the legendary crooner Leonard Cohen perform and spent the night in an altered state that had him fixating on Cohen's incredible group of backup singers. He wondered who they were and what their story was. He asked around, and no one really knew anything about them. In fact, Friesen realized, no one really knew anything about not just Cohen's but in fact about *anybody's* backup singers. Their whole world was a mystery and Friesen was fascinated. How could such talented people, who'd played such a huge part in the popular music that he'd been involved with for so many decades, be so vital and yet so invisible at the same time?

Friesen approached Neville and said, let's make a film about backup singers. Let's find out if there's a film here, and if there is, Friesen told him he'd try to get some fellow investors together to finance a documentary. Neville was, needless to say, stunned at his good fortune and soon found he was as amazed at how deeply in the shadows such pivotal figures in popular music really lived.

Neville told Friesen he'd take 3 months to research the topic, and along the way they'd figure out what their film would be about. "I went home and I put backup singers into Google, and I was shocked that there was virtually nothing. No documentaries, no books, and almost nothing in the periodicals or websites." With so little background info, Neville realized he'd just need to dive straight into doing interviews with the singers he'd heard about and simply ask them to tell him their life stories. At this point, he still had no idea what the trajectory of his film would be; so he approached the interviews as more like oral histories, simple documentation of these (mostly womens') lives. About 50 interviews later, "I started to figure out what the story might be." So he put together a 15-page treatment, gave it to Friesen, and got back the response that every documentary filmmaker covets from a funder: "Looks good to me. Let's do it."

Neville had never worked on a film in this way before, with a group of private equity investors funding it all. The budget would eventually come to "not much north of a million dollars." It wasn't a blank check by any stretch, and Neville knew full well how difficult it is to predict costs for rights-heavy music films, especially ones like this that rely on chart-toppers.

After his interviews, Neville was convinced there was definitely enough strong material on the subject to pull off a film. In fact, he felt that the story arc of just one of the backup singers he interviewed, irrepressible veteran Darlene

Love ("probably the world's most famous backup singer, a perfect oxymoron," he jokes) could easily fill a whole film.

But instead, he embraced the idea of a wide-ranging look at the lives of multiple backup singers and set out guidelines for the kinds of characters he wanted to cast. The criteria would help shape the film's tone and dynamics: amazing singers, strong characters who worked with major pop music figures, and a cross-section of women across generations to show how the backup singer lifestyle evolves over time. "I wanted to show different generations to give a sense of time passing. They'd likely have similar experiences, but they'd have made different decisions when faced with opportunities and hurdles along the way as well. I wanted to give a sense that these different women had been on a similar journey together," recalls Neville.

But the music industry is vast and complex, and backup singers work across all genres: country, heavy metal, Motown, British Invasion rock, doo wop, etc. Neville couldn't take on too many characters and risk diluting the forward motion of the film. So, from the more than 80 singers he ended up interviewing, he decided that he'd focus on just a small number of them who worked piecemeal and could sing across all genres. Darlene Love was a perfect prototype of the kind of voice-for-hire Neville was looking for: "Somebody like Darlene can sing for Buck Owens or Frank Sinatra or Frank Zappa, and nail it on the first take. She represents the best of the best who can go into a session and do anything without any chance to prepare." That is, a highly skilled freelance pro, with a superb personality and backstory—and future hopes—to share. "It was really a tall order to find a group of characters that fit all the criteria," admits Neville. But in the end, the film is dominated by a handful of such people (all women and one man), and viewers get a vivid feel for the broader common themes across the backup singer world, told via compelling individual stories.

But, deep into production, Neville would find himself in a conundrum: "I had great characters, but still no story." And they didn't really find their story until Post-Production, he says, when he settled on a three act-structure around which to drape their cross-generational tales: "All backup singers are born talented and find their way, usually accidentally, into the industry (Act One). They have these great experiences and travel with great artists and sing on great songs, and inevitably people tell them 'you're so talented, you should be doing this yourself' (Act Two). Then they make their efforts to go solo. Those all, for the most part, don't pan out for different reasons. And they ultimately have to come to terms with what they're left with in the wake of that knowledge (Act Three)."

Neville and his editor then "superimposed" their main characters' stories over this three-act framework. In this fashion Neville found a tidy and flowing structure that avoided the problem of creating a "survey"-style film, where viewers meet a stream of characters telling their stories back-to-back. Instead, Neville's main characters and "B" characters alike move through these acts chronologically, each giving her own take on how she met the challenges along the journey structure laid out by the three acts.

But for this arrangement to work without overloading viewers, it would demand a fairly lean cast. And, like so many documentary filmmakers, Neville was smitten with many of his characters. "That was the biggest challenge of all. Cutting people out of the film was the toughest thing, hands down." Sometimes he found himself equally crazy for people who had very similar stories. Often, he says, "I was in an either/or situation. I couldn't have both. I had to be really ruthless in editing."

Neville insists he left so many strong characters on the proverbial "cutting-room floor," that he's hoping the film "isn't the final word on back-up singing. I hope it's just the first word." He also worried a bit, like many filmmakers in Post, that he was trimming away lots of the historical context that surrounded these singers to keep running times down and to laser-focus on individual narratives. Though the decision to jettison this material was tough, Neville came to see that "that was a good kind of realization to come to, that I just had to take that step."

The challenge that caused the most sleepless nights for Neville and his team was the one that they'd been bracing themselves for since the beginning: securing music rights. "The first thing you need to do is nail down the rights. And the second thing you need to do is make sure the rights are nailed down. I've seen too many good documentaries never get released because of rights situations. It's so tough," he cautions.

Neville had made some previous music documentaries about artists or bands with their cooperation, and in those cases, the musician and their team are often invested in helping the filmmaker secure rights. But *Twenty Feet* was not this cozy. In fact, it was nearly the opposite: "When you're doing a film about backup singers who were always powerless in the industry, you step into their shoes"—in other words, you're just as powerless in trying to secure your rights as they were trying to secure theirs. "You're always trying to get people to do favors for you. My characters never had any leverage with the music industry, and we had no leverage with them either."

So Neville dug deep into his contacts list, and those of his music industry benefactors as well, to get help in calling in the favors they would need to secure both interviews with big name stars and clearing music rights. Producer Gil Friesen was "super tight in the music world," so he and his co-funders called, emailed, and badgered when necessary to help Neville get to the big players in music with good stories about backup singers they'd worked with. They also used "massive amounts of guilt," admits Neville, and helped snag a famously well-connected music lawyer for rights. Their full-court press delivered interviews with notoriously camera-shy stars like Bruce Springsteen and Mick Jagger, and a host of other big names like Sting and Sheryl Crow. Neville also borrowed a trick from Friesen when he was desperate to lock down a favor from someone: "Gil taught me something really valuable: always take people out to lunch, because it's much harder for people to say no to you at lunch."

Neville and his team probably racked up quite a few professional debts in assembling the starry team of interviewees and cleared songs for the film. Speaking of his benefactor Friesen, Neville says "it was so useful to have friends in high places. There's just no way this film would have happened otherwise." Even a celebrity who doesn't appear in the film played a hand. Neville recalls a story about how Friesen was one day chatting with his pal Jimmy Buffett about the film, and the "Margaritaville" legend said to Friesen: " 'Back-up singers? Yeh, they're like from twenty feet from stardom.' 'You just said it. That'll be the title,' " Friesen shot back.

Lawyer allies also helped them lock down "MFN," or Most Favored Nations clauses in their music rights agreements, which mean basically that all licensors are paid at a capped rate. That way, the negotiations are streamlined. And Neville takes special pride in using another rights tactic that would end up saving them a bundle. He and his team got rights holders to work with a "tiered" system of licensing, which addressed one of the licensors' biggest worries head on. Neville knew that "music publishers don't want to give away their songs for cheap, and then release them, the films become big hits and then they look bad because they gave away the jewels." So, Neville agreed to pay them a limited amount upfront, but he promised to pay extra if the film reached certain box office triggers. In other words, "if we do well, you do well. It's a win-win," explains Neville.

The director had had too many experiences, and knew of many others, when filmmakers end up paying music licensors fees based on optimistic revenue scenarios that don't come to pass. In effect, they're paying for rights that they don't use since their grosses fall short. In the case of *Twenty Feet*, the film performed well at the box office, and they did end up paying out "bumps" to licensors ("For some of them, I think it was the first time in history they'd ever gotten bumps from a documentary!" jokes Neville.) But if the film had tanked (sadly, a far more typical outcome for documentaries), "we would only have been committed to the money up front. The licensor wouldn't have cared, and it would have been better for us too." Neville says the strategy was a lifesaver for them, and thinks—hopes—more filmmakers will adopt the strategy when they face a film so reliant on rights holders to succeed.

Archival footage rights also proved a tough one to crack for Neville and his team. Most archival searches request the featured place or person—i.e., "Please send me footage of the Eiffel Tower.... Richard Nixon...the first Ferris wheel" etc. But those who log archival music footage never bothered to note if the material included backup singers, let alone who they were. "Every archive house told us: 'Back-up singers? We have nothing.' Of course they had stuff on backup singers, but it's just that nobody ever noticed them." So Neville's group had to scour hours and hours of footage, needle-in-a-haystack style, to find even the briefest shots of backup singers. The process often proved fruitless, labor-intensive, and of course expensive.

But Neville did find a refreshing break when it came to interviewing some of the more famous names in the film. Getting them to say yes was hard enough. And, as any filmmaker knows, famous names can be brutal to interview— reciting rote lines about their next project, holding back way more than they're giving, or just generally having about as much fun in the interview chair as in a dentist's chair. But when it came to interviewing them about backup singers, their response was a relief. It went like this: the star would sit down and right away apologize for not having anything to say about backup singers ("I haven't thought about it that much.") But as soon as they got started, it turned out they had loads to say about backup singers. "It's people that they've worked with and known and loved, in many cases for decades. They had just never thought about it...," says Neville.

In the film, the likes of Sting and Bruce Springsteen do seem genuinely engaged in talking about people and issues they only *thought* they'd ignored. In one especially memorable scene, Neville plays for both Mick Jagger and backup singer Merry Clayton an audio track he'd unearthed from the Stones' towering "Gimme Shelter"—Clayton's haunting, soaring vocals ("Rape...! Murder...! It's just a shot away, just a shot away..."). The backup track stands alone—without Jagger's classic "Gimme Shelter" wrapped around it. The room stands empty too. No question hanging in the air, just reaction shots from both Jagger and Clayton, inter-cut, as they take in—for the first time— Clayton's work unadorned. Clayton is tickled and flattered, while Jagger seems downright amazed at the potency of his hired hand's magnificent sonic power.

In fact, Neville realizes, it turns out that "nobody understands the backup singer better than the lead singer. The leads should be grateful to them and they are." The stars speak about backups they actually knew and worked with, not in abstractions. Sting even takes the conversation to a fascinating plane that's surprising coming from a man of his ego. Explaining why he's on one side of the main mic, and these blazing talents toil in the shadows on the other side of it, Sting likened his experience to a form of "survivor's guilt," as in, "I just happen to be the guy that won the lottery this time," noted Neville.

These kinds of insights tell us both about the people making them and about those whom they are referencing. What becomes clear watching *Twenty Feet* is that none of the backups profiled lack for talent. Their singing is superb, occasionally sublime and sometimes even better than the singers they are supporting. The problem is that the stars have heapings of the key ingredient that most backups lack—laser-focused ambition. "They are insanely talented people, but they're not necessarily the most ambitious or the luckiest... They don't have that Madonna thing. You know, 'I'll crawl over broken glass to become famous,'" says Neville.

The director shapes the final act of the film around this idea. "That's really the point of the film, which is, it's not about becoming famous or not making it. It's about what happens when you don't achieve your dreams... Sometimes just doing the work is its own reward... The film is about making peace with the life you have, and the life you dreamt of having."

And Neville employs a clever device to underscore the virtually impossible odds that his characters face when trying to assert their musical identities. Neville puts brightly colored dots and splotches over the womens' faces as they appear on a series of album covers and performance stills panning by. These people are—figuratively and literally—just not in the picture.

There is, though, one fascinating stretch of the film when one of these perennial bridesmaids does assert herself, in a surprising fashion. Merry Clayton is asked to sing backup for the notorious Southern redneck band, Lynyrd Skynyrd. Their song, "Sweet Home Alabama," is the last word in Confederate pride for a band that plastered its live shows and album covers with the rebel flag. At first, Clayton puts her foot down, wanting nothing to do with the message or the messengers. But her much older husband, a veteran musician on the scene, took the long view and urged Clayton to defy the good ole boys by saying yes instead. She complies, and the footage is mesmerizing. As we watch her sing, we wonder, is she just doing her job to pay the bills, or is she symbolically raising her middle finger by raising her voice?

"Her husband told her, 'show your strength instead of just saying no.' You're doing the best work you can, and that's empowering," is how Neville sees Clayton's choice. "If you're a brilliant and strong black voice, regardless of the context, you're making a statement of racial pride."

Clayton's remarkable and unusual act of defiance is a hallmark of Neville's cast of characters. Feisty, warm, endearing and driven women blessed with perfect pipes trying to make it in an industry that always seems to want just a little bit more from them, just a little bit something ... else. He would shoot them throughout most of 2011, spend much of the next year in Post, and then apply to Sundance in the fall of 2012. Acceptance came soon after. But just after the euphoria of getting in to Sundance, tragedy struck. Neville's patron Gil Friesen, and the man who got the project off the ground, died in December of that year from leukemia, just weeks before its Park City premiere in January 2013.

But despite the tragedy, Sundance would seal the film's fairy tale journey. Friesen's constellation of family and friends turned up in Utah, helping to rally support for the film that had made Friesen so proud. And the backup singer stars called him repeatedly in Utah with prayers. After carefully keeping the film secret until its premiere, a scene unfolded that was right out of, well, a movie...Several studios bid frantically for rights after its premiere, and Neville's team and his agents condo-hopped through the wee hours. By 5.00 a.m., Harvey Weinstein's company emerged from the scrum with a distribution deal in place. "Gil's death just before Sundance added so much emotionally to the whole event. And then the way we sold it was crazy—an incredible experience...Like a dream," recalls Neville.

But before hitting the theatrical circuit, Neville had to run *Twenty Feet* past the Film Ratings Board, not expecting much of a problem. But the verdict was a bad one—an "R" rating. Neville wanted older children to see the film and families too. An R could be it's commercial undoing. But the Board had a solution—drop one of your three uses of the "F Word," and get rid of the naked breast on that Playboy cover, and you'll get a PG-13. So, blurry went the breast, and his editor performed microscopic audio surgery to swap out one of the F words for a less offensive curse. After the operation, voila—"PG-13."

A Best Documentary Feature Oscar nomination would come later that year. And with it, his first contact with the studio head who bought the rights to his film back at Sundance. "Congratulations, Morgan," the email said. "So proud of you. Now the hard work begins." By "hard work," Weinstein meant the requisite lobbying that every Oscar nominee undergoes. Perhaps it worked, because in early 2014, *Twenty Feet* won the Oscar, capping off an outrageous ride that Neville could scarcely fathom. In fact, he says, every best case dream scenario he nurtured for the film—came to pass.

Since then, broadcasters and funders "are offering me docs right and left. It's opened up so many doors. It's really nice." He's developing some narrative projects too, and things look rosy indeed. The irony is not lost on Neville that a film about unheralded talents would pave the way for his and his characters' own starry futures. "I feel like my journey and the journey of my singers in the film were one and the same. We'd all been in (our fields) for a long time, and we all felt the time was right, and we did the best work we could and people liked it."

In ruminating over some of the magical moments that have followed the release of *Twenty Feet*, there's one glorious incident one night after a screening that still brings a head shake and a wide smile to Neville's eyes. "A guy stood up and said, 'I'm a middle manager at a software company and I work with a team of people. I'm really proud of the work we do. But I don't get all the money and credit in the world and I'm okay with that. I realized tonight that … *I'm* the backup singer. We're *all* backup singers!'"

5

Spellbound

DIRECTOR AND PRODUCER

Jeffrey Blitz

Oscar Nomination, 2002

SUMMARY

Follows a group of youthful competitors from around the country as they head to the Scripps National Spelling Bee in Washington, D.C.

Spellbound is a tight, riveting, and emotional roller-coaster ride through a world most of us probably haven't given a lot of thought to since around 4th grade—the spelling bee.

It's the peculiar genius of director Jeffrey Blitz to have taken an ultra-simple framework—who's going to win the bee?—and turned it into the complex, layered confection that earned it an Oscar nomination, hefty profits and the lasting affections of both adult and child fans. The International Documentary Association called *Spellbound* one of the top five documentaries ever made.

Even more impressive? It was his very first documentary. And, like many novices, the path to making *Spellbound* was so riddled with mis-steps, massive debts, and luck (both good and bad) that Blitz still shakes his head at the thought of it today.

The New Jersey native found himself, in the late 1990s, like a lot of people in his situation right after graduating from film school at University of Southern California School of Cinematic Arts : pumped full of knowledge but drained of cash. At USC he was known for his "gritty and edgy" short narratives, he says. Blitz describes his best graduate school work as a "dark, really (messed) up, David Lynch-y film" that earned him some Hollywood meetings and might, just might, eventually land him a straight-to-video deal.

"It was such a horrifying thought to me after imagining myself to be a more independent-minded filmmaker with a voice that I would suddenly have to make stuff that I thought was really crappy," he now recalls.

Not only that, but it would feel like "a job"—a concept that had always aroused Blitz's anxieties. "I don't mind commercially-minded, but this stuff wasn't worth my time. And I'm just not good at doing things that I don't really enjoy doing."

Around that time, Blitz had stumbled across an ESPN special about the Scripps National Spelling Bee. Amazed by the bee's high drama and stakes, he set out to write a narrative script inspired by it. But then, a harsh realization set in. "Even if I wrote a really perfect script, the chances that anyone would really let me make this, and the chance that anyone would let me have the creative autonomy I wanted to have, were almost nil."

The elements that Blitz craved—creative control and a small enough crew to ensure the auteur's imprint on every frame—all pointed him in a very different direction: documentary.

Telling the spelling bee as a documentary, he realized, had some built-in advantages. "I could get myself a camera, I could find a friend who knows how to record sound, and could be a total one-man band, entirely self-reliant." This appealed to his inner control freak, even though he'd focused mostly on narrative films while in school. "It really represented a pragmatic choice more than a value of documentary as a forum over fiction," he confesses.

And thus, bumpily, a documentary is born. Blitz finds himself in 1999 atop the (low-end, Sam's Club) director's chair, in possession of a decent idea and zero funds. In graduate school he'd taken a documentary editing class, which he hoped would give some directing guidance in the field. He'd also have to transfer lessons from the narrative classes he took while at USC into making a documentary.

His lack of budget and obsession with control conspired to guide key production decisions. "Even though I'm not the best cinematographer in the world, I'm going to have to shoot it, because I don't want to have to bargain with a cinematographer" he says. Once he found a producing partner to make the film with, his friend Sean Welch, he would do the job Blitz could live with micro-managing less: sound.

Control would even trump production values. If hiring a less experienced shooter (himself) meant sacrificing visual flair, then so be it. If he hired a veteran shooter, "it may be that the movie is better … but the experience of making the movie wouldn't be better for me."

Ditto with lights. He simply doesn't use them, opting for authenticity over manicured looks. To Blitz, it's as much an aesthetic decision as one about the power dynamic between the interviewer and the interviewee. His rationale is that "what you get out of that person feeling like she has invited me into her world instead of I have come and changed her world to suit my needs … I just don't believe that kind of trade off is worth it for the kinds of films I'm making."

As far as the cameras, it would be catch as catch can—a motley selection of mini-DV rigs, in the hands of many of his friends. If formats or technical specifications didn't mesh, so be it. He knew that any friend with a camera and even the barest skills would have to be summoned if he was to pull this off.

On *Spellbound*, he would just have to hope that viewers would be so captivated by the drama of the story and the characters, that they'd overlook, or at least forgive, the technical flaws, however preventable they may have been.

But first, he'd have to figure out how to tackle the many-headed beast that is the Scripps National Spelling Bee and the countless local bees that funnel the whiz kid spellers to the championship. The Bee has about 270 contestants. Theoretically, any one of them could win. How to be sure he'd be following spellers who might have a crack at making it to the championship or even making it to a later round or winning? Or would spotlighting the winner or even driving the narrative toward a victor even make sense? These are questions that Blitz would struggle with for the next four years while he made the film.

Lacking money, he turned to the (quasi) free line item that has salvaged so many documentaries—time. In 1998, he had found himself working at the Writer's Guild, doing research on the Hollywood blacklist. But in every bit of down time, he'd research spelling bees. He immersed himself in bee arcana. He studied past winners and losers, studied the words they won and choked on, and consulted legions of bee scouts and coaches.

He cooked up endless "complicated and ridiculous formulas" to try to game that world. In order to pull off the shoot with no funding, he needed to try to figure out where it was wisest to throw his scant resources. If not, he'd run the risk of chasing down contestants across the country and blowing his money long before the final "ding" of the judge's bell that signals an incorrectly spelled word.

But clever research could only take him so far. At some point, somebody's got to hit the road and begin shooting—and spending. Credit cards would have to finance *Spellbound*. "We financed the whole thing on credit card. We would literally max out on credit cards, come home, wait for a moment when it was easier to get credit cards, apply for a new one, and go hit the road again until it was maxed ... "

It was a high-risk move and an acute source of anxiety during the whole production. He likens the feeling to "a frog being boiled slowly. Painful, and not quick. It's really a disastrous way (to finance a film)." His head was filled with a roll-call of friends who'd recently racked up mountains of debt "to produce phenomenal movies that no one will see." Despite ruthless cost-cutting on the road, by the time he'd finished producing *Spellbound*, they had maxed out more than a dozen different credit cards. A sympathetic brother with a cushy TV writing gig paid down his debts during one particularly hairy stretch, but that just created for Blitz a new paymaster.

Luckily for Blitz, he recalls with a smile, his parents were not in the film industry. "They didn't really understand how irresponsible this was!"

To try to winnow down his shooting, he "handicapped" the talent, using formulas he cooked up. Any kid who went far the previous year but lost on a very hard word—in. Kids who had siblings who did really well the previous year, possibly forming the nucleus of a spelling dynasty? In.

But of course, that would still leave dozens of potential stars uncovered. So for those spellers he wasn't targeting before the bee, he realized he'd almost certainly have to do plenty of shooting after the bee. He hoped to have to move around sequences like this as little as possible, because this presented an ethical dilemma: is it okay to shoot post-bee material as if it was happening before the bee?

When he started shooting material with characters who he'd missed but who shone at the bee, he wasn't certain how he'd use that material. "I wasn't smart enough to have figured out how I was going to structure it. But ultimately we cut it in to the film with the idea that it actually just fits, and we're not going to make a big deal about exactly when it happened. ... what can you do, you know?"

So, for example, if he uncovers someone at the championship with a compelling story and who goes into deeper rounds, he can go back to his or her house after the event, and film scenes not pegged to any particular period of time, like them studying or walking to school. But he draws the line at re-creations. "I would have never thought to say, 'show me what it was like to practice,' for example." But the question of shooting out of sequence always loomed large for Blitz.

With so many potential pitfalls in the film's planning, perhaps it was inevitable that the very first character Blitz decided to film, ended up a bust. He and his soundman flew to St. Louis to interview a boy called Georgie, who Blitz had a very strong hunch was going to win the whole bee. But it was the first documentary shooting Blitz had ever done and his amateurism showed, badly. "I didn't know what I was doing at all. We didn't know where we were going with this, we stayed in the worst hotel in East St. Louis and the whole thing was just ridiculous." After half a day of disastrous shooting, Georgie's parents basically tossed them out of the house and told them to go away. "I would've bet a lot of money that Georgie was going to win the bee that year. I was, like, 'O man, our winning story is gone. What are we going to do?'"

But instead of walking away, a despondent Blitz gazed out a little further into the Missouri farm country around him and decided to follow another hunch. He heard about a farmer's son who lived about three hours away and who fit some of Blitz's criteria—a promising speller, and his brother had gone deep in the bee the year before. Best of all, the boy's regional tournament was coming up and if he won, he'd go to the championship in Washington, D.C. They shot him for about a week, but in the regional bee, their man got beat. "Oh my god, the movie's dead" was Blitz's first reaction after that hellish first week.

After licking his wounds a bit, Blitz and his partner knew they needed a score. They needed to film someone who was a compelling character and who could win in the regionals. He'd heard a tip about a girl named Angela Arenivar from Amarillo, Texas, whose parents didn't speak English but who was studying hard. He couldn't gauge her tournament prospects but decided to throw a different lens onto Angela: "That's a great human interest story whether or not she makes it." Not necessarily a rising "star" in the bee universe but a compelling, unusual story nonetheless.

Blitz's hunch would pay off. "Angela's bee lasts forever, and she won, and Sean and I actually put down our equipment and started hugging, because we felt like, ok, we're going to have a movie. Up until that moment, we didn't know if we would or not. Her victory was as much for us as for her."

Angela's tale is riveting and her story opens up *Spellbound*. Her bee victory only caps off a string of much more intimate and deeper challenges she has to wrestle with every day. The ranch owners on whose farm her family lives and works back-handedly compliment her as an example of a "good Mexican." Her faraway father is noted to speak more often to his cows than to his family, and she is seen watching a television newscast about the powers-that-be wrestling matter of factly with the fate of immigrants like herself. Viewers who aren't weeping at her bee win are simply not paying attention.

By the time the championship in Washington is about to start, Blitz has a handful of Angela-caliber stories under his belt. Phase 1 of production is done, and Blitz is feeling optimistic. But then a new hurdle: the Bee organizers tell Blitz they don't want him to shoot the event, and they try to shut down production. Blitz panics and tries desperately to persuade them to change their mind. But while he's trying to negotiate his return, he hears about yet more promising spellers with compelling stories. So, instead of just fretting about Bee access, he decides to think positively and expand the pool of contestants, summons friends to help shoot, and they all go out and harvest more stories. Ultimately, this decision will turn out to be a life-saver, because it gives Blitz more options for Post-Production in case his initial group of spellers flames out early. And the Bee organizers would of course end up changing their minds and allowing him access.

For both practical and aesthetic reasons, Blitz says he always wanted to downplay the obvious through line of: "who's going to win?" He told himself that "the movie can seem like such a good hearted movie by saying the winning is less important than letting these kids share their lives." Idealistic, yes, and sweet, but at the same time he knew in his gut that "if all the kids had gone down in the early rounds, I think I would've just abandoned the footage" and tried again the following year. "An enormously expensive exercise." He knew he needed to have "multiple spellers going pretty deep in competition in order for the movie to work." Thanks to a mix of overcaution and overshooting, he would meet that threshold.

But downplaying the path to victory also posed risks, because that structural through line gives Blitz a built-in "architecture" for the whole film that he relishes. "There's a clear beginning, middle and end to it … it's easy to see the scaffolding for that. For a lot of other documentaries, it just feels like you're brought into a world and it's very invisible how it's structured." In the end, Blitz decides that he has to embrace this built-in narrative framework and figure out ways to make the characters more compelling than their ultimate plight in the championship.

But settling on that editing approach and sifting through the many hours of footage meant he didn't bring on an editor until a year after shooting finished. His mentor at USC, veteran editor Kate Amend, suggested a teaching assistant there to cut *Spellbound* with Blitz. No nonsense, Russian-born Yana Gorskaya would become Blitz's "indelible partner" for this and several of his next films, including the narrative *Rocket Science* (2007) and *Lucky* (2010). She and Blitz emerged from the same academic milieu, each was strong-willed, and Blitz valued not only her creative input but also a "mothering presence" that boosted morale.

Their first cut was a nearly three-hour stem-winder that Blitz calls, jokingly, "a masterpiece." His mentor told him otherwise, saying it was way too long, and Blitz eventually came around to her point of view.

One of the most difficult aspects of the story to deal with in Post was the question of how to handle Speller #8, the ineffable and highly quirky boy from New Jersey named Harry Altman. Blitz's team noticed at the championship that the kinetic Harry, with his wildly elastic facial muscles and wise-cracking ways, was the center of attention among his fellow contestants. Nobody seemed to be able to take their eyes off Harry. Blitz hadn't shot with him before the championship but decided on the spot that no matter how Harry fared, he had to go back to shoot him at home.

By odd coincidence, Harry and Blitz's home lives overlapped. Harry lived in the next town over from Ridgewood, New Jersey, Blitz's hometown. Blitz's mom had once been Harry's doctor, and Blitz knew Harry's life intimately—it was nearly his own.

But Blitz worried that Harry's deeply quirky gestures, un-funny jokes, and jangly ways would open Harry up to ridicule. "The first cuts that Yana did, I didn't even have her watch the Harry tapes, because I just thought it's going to be very hard to do without having him be just someone who kids are laughing at." But Yana disagreed, telling Blitz he was being over sensitive and too politically correct and that in fact she thinks that Harry could be portrayed in a frank way that could make him "the contestant that people really root for."

Luckily for viewers ever since, Yana won that bet. Harry is the character who lingers in your mind for days and weeks after watching the film. He provides a penetrating glimpse into the unadorned thoughts of this most delicate and volatile age group. He tosses back any pity we might have sent his way and fills us with joy and amazement. The spelling bee format itself comes to feel way too tame a venue to assess Harry's rangy, sinewy charms.

After Blitz completed the film in 2002, it enjoyed a buoyant festival run and then got picked up for theatrical release by Think Film. *Spellbound* found a fan in Greg Daniels, who helped create the American version of the hit TV series "The Office," and a few years later, Daniels offered Blitz a gig directing an episode. One of the dozen or so episodes of "The Office" that Blitz would end up directing had the good fortune to run right after the 2009 Super Bowl, had huge viewership numbers, and won Blitz an Emmy for Direction, Best Comedy Series.

Despite all the adulation over the years, Blitz still muses over a persistent criticism in one scene of the film. Fans often ask him about a scene at the end where we see Nupur Lala, the eventual champion, seeming to gloat, champion-like, before she has spelled her winning word. People have complained that that out-of-sequence scene seems to suck the energy out of the win. Blitz has a ready answer: "We did that deliberately because we wanted to signal to the audience that ultimately wining was not important. And if you thought that it was, we wanted you to be able to believe that all the way up to the very end..."

6

The Act of Killing

DIRECTOR AND PRODUCER

Joshua Oppenheimer

Best Documentary Feature, Oscar Nomination 2013

SUMMARY

This shocking and magnificent experimental film explores the lives of unrepentant former killers in Indonesia, who gleefully act out their crimes for the benefit of the cameras.

The way Joshua Oppenheimer describes it, it sounds like the worst kind of dream. "I had this awful feeling that I'd wandered into Germany 40 years after the Holocaust only to find the Nazis still in power." But Oppenheimer was wide awake, and the nightmare has lasted half a century. And it's completely true. The twisted fruits of Oppenheimer's long fever dream live on in his spellbinding film, *The Act of Killing*.

There aren't many productions where the director opens interviews by asking: "So, you've participated in one of the biggest killings in human history. Let's talk about that ..." And in *The Act of Killing*, mass killers do just that, laying on details and even dramatically reprising their crimes for Oppenheimer. "I was that open with them because they were that open with me: 'How do you see yourself? How do you live with this, and make sense of this?' " recalls Oppenheimer.

The engine that drives Oppenheimer's haunting film is the question of impunity. What happens to a society, in this case Indonesia, where mass killers not only roam free, but are rewarded with top jobs in government and business since committing their crimes half a century ago? There are no Nuremberg-style prosecutors hunting them down. In fact, the opposite is true. The killers openly celebrate their crimes, with zero risk of apprehension.

The seeds of *The Act of Killing* began to germinate in 2001. The Texas-born Oppenheimer was living on the island of Sumatra in Indonesia, helping a group of filmmakers to produce a documentary about palm oil workers who were trying to unionize and agitate for better working conditions. Conditions for the workers were deplorable, featuring a cesspool of toxic chemicals, appalling pay, and breakneck schedules. The chemicals were sickening and killing many of the workers he encountered, and he was enraged. "My friends were being killed making margarine, basically," as he sums up the grisly toll of the palm oil plantations.

Oppenheimer was incensed to see how, whenever any of the workers asked for even simple protective gear or any improvements, employers would hire young thugs to harass and attack them. He found out that this brutal dynamic had prevailed since 1965, the year when a failed coup led to a ruthless anticommunist purge across Indonesia, and the government hired gangsters to jail and kill anyone suspected of any ties to unions. They murdered more than half a million people in barely a year.

"The workers' parents and grandparents had been in a strong plantation workers union until 1965. They had been accused of being potential communist sympathizers simply for being in the union and had been killed. But the perpetrators were still in power all around the workers. I'd even call the workers 'survivors.' They lived with the fear that this could happen to them too and remained suppressed," explains Oppenheimer. The film he was helping to make, called *The Globalization Tapes*, explores these dynamics. When it was finished in 2003, Oppenheimer wanted to find out more about the contours and social impact of these popular fears, a journey that would eventually lead to *The Act of Killing*.

He was stunned by the numbing paralysis that thwarted any hope of progress for so many Indonesian workers, especially those on Sumatra, a hotbed of anticommunist suppression since 1965. His *Globalization* subjects urged him on too. "Come back here to Sumatra, and let's make another film about why we're afraid," they asked him. So for the next seven years, from 2003 to 2010, Oppenheimer shuttled back and forth between London and Sumatra to explore these issues.

What really struck him was how "the killers' total impunity creates the fear that this can happen again. The victor's history, the story the regime tells justifying what it did, becomes a tool of suppression today. Story telling becomes a tool, an instrument of terror, you may even say." Oppenheimer hoped his film would relate a very different story. He wanted to turn the official story on its head and reveal the lies that undergird it.

So he first attempted to interview the victims, those living with these fears. But the fears that silenced villagers would stop Oppenheimer as well. As soon as the Army, stationed in every village in Indonesia, found out what Oppenheimer was up to, they began to threaten survivors. So Oppenheimer had to stop. But he wasn't about to give up, and decided to try the opposite tack. He wondered if he could interview the perpetrators themselves about their actions during the murderous years of 1965–1966 and, by extension, perhaps shed some light on how the fears they sowed then still remain. It was a roll of the dice. Would the killers be candid? Would they turn on him and threaten him? He decided to just plunge in and find out.

"I was afraid to approach them, but when I did I found to my horror that every single one of them was immediately open, and immediately boastful about the worst details of the killings, which they would recount with smile on their faces and in front of their families and even small grandchildr recalls Oppenheimer.

Off and on for the next two years, from 2003 to 2005, he went from village to village, camera in hand, to interview mass killers. He would end up interviewing more than forty of them. He traveled light, solo or with a lean crew, and by then was even fluent in Indonesian, which he'd picked up during the *Globalization* film. "Astonished, disturbed and horrified" is how he describes his state of mind after those encounters. "Typically they would open up immediately when I met them, and then they would invite me to the places where they killed, and launch into spontaneous demonstrations on how they did it," recalls Oppenheimer, still seeming a little shaken even years later. Often they'd bring favored killing tools like machetes, spades, wire and other props. Some brought friends, families along—just another day in the park. The normalcy of it all made Oppenheimer's blood curdle.

After two numbing years in the throes of murder and madness, Oppenheimer met an ex-killer who took him into uncharted territory. His name was Anwar Congo, perpetrator number 41. Like many others, Congo brought a friend along, took Oppenheimer to his favored murder spot, and gave a killing demonstration. And after the demonstration, a little dance. One of his favorites: the "cha-cha-cha." But then Congo shared something with the filmmaker that he'd not heard before: "I have nightmares. I go out drinking and dancing my whole life to forget these things." Congo spoke of mental anguish and acute pain and of wanting to run away from that pain. None of Congo's predecessors had expressed these kinds of sentiments before.

To Oppenheimer, it was a revelation. "I had this sudden realization that trauma, if not guilt too, are involved in the creation image of a man dancing when he's killed hundreds of people ... his dancing became a metaphor for impunity, for the victory of the killers." But was Congo shimmying to remember or to forget? To banish pain or to summon it? Anwar Congo's cauldron of conflict represented an epiphany for Oppenheimer. And soon, Congo would e over his film.

Perhaps, thought Oppenheimer, Congo was simply verbalizing an anguish that the others felt as well but could not verbalize. Perhaps all the boasting and apparent glee the killers shared with him represented not joy but a malignant giddiness that had simply never been ethically challenged? Maybe their swagger was closer to performance than testimony? "Suddenly, I realized," says Oppenheimer, "that boasting and remorse could be two sides of the same coin." These thoughts set Oppenheimer's mind racing, and now he was mentally reassessing all of his encounters with the Sumatran killers over the past two years.

He decided to try an experiment with Congo, to test this brewing hypothesis further. He decided to screen for Congo the footage of his interview with him. "I did that because I needed to know: is he disassociating? Will he recognize the horror that he's just talked about when he watches it? ... If he and they are performing, who is the audience? How do they want to be seen, and how do they see themselves?"

Screening Congo's interview for him was enormously risky. Congo, like many of the other killers, still had a vast web of contacts with the Army and police. Angering him could have led to swift arrest or worse. Just before screening, Oppenheimer sent a brave production manager to the airport, with cash, to buy them tickets to instantly flee Indonesia if needed. If she didn't get an "all-clear" text message by an appointed time, she was to buy the tickets.

Right after showing him the footage, Oppenheimer feared the worst. "Anwar looked very disturbed," he recalls. Congo's first comments came as a shock: "My hair is all wrong ... my clothes are all wrong. My acting is bad ... " Congo, Oppenheimer realized, was clinging to the multiplicity of lies that had gotten him to his torn up state in the first place. It wasn't that these thespian confessions *were* bad. They just *looked* bad. "He looks at the footage as if, if he can just fix the scene aesthetically, maybe he can make it better for himself morally too."

Oppenheimer decided to continue the experiment, hoping Congo's reflections on the footage might get them to psychological insights they couldn't have otherwise attained. He'd shoot, they'd screen, over and over. Along the way, Congo opened up more about his nightmares, rages, and ragged feelings. Oppenheimer reciprocated and emerged from these encounters with a fresh epiphany about his film: he'd spent two years looking for monsters but then realized to his intense discomfort that what he was searching for all along were simply—people. "With Anwar, I finally saw a human being.... I've refused to make the leap from saying he's a man who's done something monstrous, to he's a monster."

So, most of the next five years, 2005–2010, Oppenheimer spent filming Anwar Congo. They both now saw dramatic methods as vital to the enterprise. To help discover Congo's inner truths, they'd examine not just his words and deeds but also the way he re-spun his emotions in dramatically recreated settings outside himself. In an unusual twist in a tale already overcrowded with them, Congo was, like many Indonesians, smitten with Hollywood films. His love for Hollywood dated all the way back to his years as a killer-for-hire in the mid-60s, when he worked in ticket rackets at Sumatran movie theaters.

Cowboy movies, cheesy musicals, gangster movies, war epics—Congo loved them all. And much of *The Act of Killing*, in fact partly the source of its title, involves Congo and his fellows filming scenes that dramatize their killings on improvised Hollywood-style movie sets. Oppenheimer encouraged Congo to imagine appropriate scenes and action, and together they found writers to write scripts, television stations to provide studio space, and crew to help shoot. Oppenheimer picked up the costs for the scenes. "We of course funded the scenes since they were only existing for our movie." They kept costs to a minimum by calling in favors whenever they could, and made clear to the men that the scenes they were making were solely intended for *The Act of Killing* and were not going to end up in any separate stand-alone film. They were set as closer to therapeutic filmed exercises than for any theatrical legacy.

And Oppenheimer imposed strict limits on matters of taste and ethics. He had to put his foot down on some of Congo's filming requests. This happened on occasions when Congo wanted to, for example, recreate lavish attack scenes in the very locations where he and fellow gangsters had actually committed them. No, too close to home. Sometimes Congo would propose a scene that was completely made up—a chase scene, for example. Can't do it, said Oppenheimer: amusement for its own sake was not the point of these exercises. But when Oppenheimer felt like a scene Congo proposed might shed important insights, and was financially within reason, he was inclined to "greenlight," so to speak, since he felt that going through with the scenes were yielding critical insights into Congo's psyche.

One of the more difficult ethical dilemmas involving the "film within a film" device was recreating a village massacre Congo's youthful gang of thugs had pulled off during the purges and of which they were very proud. Oppenheimer insisted that they draw the actors for the reenactment only from perpetrators or their immediate families—no outsiders. The battle scene lasts a long time and is exceedingly brutal and disturbing to watch, on many levels. And Oppenheimer concedes that "real trauma" comes up in the scene, such as with the real life wife of an ex-killer with the blood of possibly hundreds on his hands. "The trauma of being a perpetrator's wife ... she uses the scene as a safe space to express some of these feelings."

Sometimes, before, after or even during staged scenes, Oppenheimer and Congo would duck away from the narrative film around them and quietly continue on with their straight documentary shooting, getting him to reflect in the context of his scene-making. At one point, a crony of Congo's begs him to end a scene that he worries is becoming is too close to a criminal confession and might make them "look bad." But Congo begs him off. In one (un)fun house mirror-like scene, Congo plays the victim to his own crimes and comes emotionally undone. Guilt? Remorse? Too gentle? Too rough? Poor acting? It is, of course, really impossible to tell.

In the bizarre rabbit hole that the film was becoming, the macabre twists on Hollywood they were filming would even reshape Oppenheimer's own take on cinema. "Once Anwar proposed a cowboy scene based on a genocide. Of course it's tasteless and absurd, until I recognized that the cowboy genre itself came into being to glorify genocide. It's the way we glorified and lied about the killing of Native Americans. I started seeing a lot of how *we* use cinema in how Anwar was trying to use cinema."

Oppenheimer would film Congo and company in full costume and make-up in a range of settings—mass village battle scenes, dingy offices turned torture dungeons, and an indelible scene of the men accompanied by dancers and singing "Born Free" under a towering waterfall. The tableau are surreal in the extreme, and it's hard to imagine viewers not lurching from horror to bafflement to repugnance in the same instant. Oppenheimer succinctly sums up the kinky Hollywood-on-its-head devices that propel his film: "the whole filming project was this kind of unbelievable, glowing, toxic mutant metaphor for impunity."

Viewers are challenged and jarred wildly for much of Oppenheimer's film, with remarkable and disturbing scenes stacked up end to end. No real heroes. Just puzzles. No real answers. And even the questions are baffling. Though he's intent on exposing the deep and longstanding corruption of the Indonesian regime, he denies viewers any clear path to help make this unfold. This would be, to him, oversimplifying. "It's all an exploration," he says. "My moral responsibility is to pose the most important questions that each situation involves." Easy answers are swatted away. "If I know the story I'm going to tell when I'm shooting, then I shouldn't be shooting that story." He tosses viewers high into the air and lets them figure out how to get themselves back down. He set himself up clear signposts for when to finish as well. "When you're no longer getting deeper, and you're just getting more stuff, or you start drifting laterally … then you're done shooting that film."

More than 1,200 hours of footage later, Oppenheimer was ready to start folding up shooting and to begin editing in earnest. What would he create? He wasn't exactly sure but felt sure he could deliver "an experience." He wanted to show that Anwar had "come to terms with something," but he didn't know exactly what. The material Oppenheimer had to edit with was both voluminous and vexing. On the one hand, the material had an odd Russian doll quality to it, where scenes sometimes fit into bigger frameworks and yet again into others. And there was the surreal nature to the overlapping narratives living inside documentary material, and vice versa, in addition to scenes for a "film within film" running quasi-parallel to the straight documentary material. "There was mountains of footage, and I really had to just try to excavate the layers of material," Oppenheimer says of the multi-year Post-Production schedule.

He knew from the outset that, no matter how outrageous, he wanted to reckon with every character and view every scene at face value and without adding any extra layer of commentary, however subtle. It was an "observational documentary of the imagination," as Oppenheimer calls it. Much of the material would have been laughably easy to ridicule and on which to cast judgment—taboo for Oppenheimer.

A perfect example is the scene at the waterfall where Congo and company act out moments from their crimes and are greeted by "angels" in heaven, while singing Andy Williams' kitsch liberation anthem, "Born Free." "We intellectually know that scene is grotesque and absurd, and it would have been easy to look down on them and sneer ... but I made the decision to make it look as powerful and beautiful as possible, just as Anwar imagined it," says Oppenheimer. He recognized that he had an extravagance of outrageous material, and it would have been easy to crank up its inherent power and drama even more, but he decided to go in the other direction and deliver it to viewers unadorned. This way, the audience is more engaged, left to themselves to decipher the aesthetic and ethical messes unfolding before them.

And Oppenheimer wanted to explore his unusual mountain of material in as many ways as he could. After finishing a cut of *The Act of Killing*, he cut another shorter version for American and other audiences. He'd also go back to Indonesia to get material for yet one more film altogether, knowing that after *The Act of Killing* came out that he'd likely never be able to safely return to Indonesia. He says the second film, called *The Look of Silence*, is not a sequel but "the second in a pair, a diptych if you like. I hope they're shown side by side eventually." He and his crew were so afraid of repercussions after *The Act of Killing* came out that many of the closing credits read "Anonymous."

But shooting so much material, and working on two continents, wasn't cheap. He had first tapped into a stipend he was getting for a PhD he was working on through Central Saint Martins College of Art and Design in London. When those funds ran out, he tapped a government research grant in the United Kingdom. Then, a Danish producer, Signe Byrge Sorensen, came in and raised funds from European film institutes, NGOs, and numerous broadcasters. In the latter stages, documentary heavyweights including Werner Herzog and Errol Morris helped draw attention to the film as well.

But even after Oppenheimer left Indonesia, the horrors he unearthed there followed him home. He discovered he could never really leave. The frightening insights and experiences left him feeling isolated and desolate. "It was alienating going home to London with this material that no one around me knew or even cared about." And, since he was still working off of academic funding with no real timetable, there was no production company or broadcaster who might have asked for dailies, pushed him into deadlines and perhaps helped him channel his torn feelings into a clear work mission. Once home, Oppenheimer was on his own and still psychologically trying to rebuild himself.

He was trying to recover from a terrible time during filming when he simply went into a free fall. He traces his descent back to a moment with Congo that seared his conscience as almost no other. It's a scene where Congo, dressed in a gangster suit, viciously butchers a teddy bear. "He was showing perhaps how he killed children, or maybe it's just a game, an improvisation ... it's hard to know," he recalls. When Oppenheimer had to go over to Congo to adjust his mic during the scene, Congo noticed that the director was crying. "I hadn't noticed I was crying. In fact, it's the only time in my life where I've been crying without realizing it. And Anwar said, 'What should we do?' And I said, well, we should continue." The moment scarred him to the nub and led to eight months straight of horrible nightmares. "I felt like we had been complicit in a crime just by going into that horror ... I wouldn't be able to sleep because of the memories of the nightmares from the previous night. The next night, it would start again." He says an alarming percentage of the film was shot with literally zero sleep—for days on end.

Part of the psychic pain stemmed from the film's unusually dark vantage point—boring into the mind-set of an unrepentant killer, without the solace of a hero or solution anywhere in sight. Many human rights-oriented films hitch a ride onto a prosecutor or investigator-type for this kind of exploration. There are clear good guys and bad guys. To Oppenheimer, that's understandable. "That's a comfortable way to approach these kinds of people. It's safer ... and we can identify with someone we like." Not so for *The Act of Killing*. Pretty much every one confounds and repulses us.

For viewers, the ordeal of the film can be grueling indeed. For the filmmaker, multiple times more so, but it was an experience that would leave Oppenheimer with a powerful and sober new outlook on the Congos, the Hitlers, the Jeffrey Dahmers among us. Oppenheimer hopes viewers come away from his film not viewing Congo as a separate and evil life-form, but as a human being just like the rest of us. "I hope viewers see Anwar's humanity. Not to think like him, but to recognize themselves in some small part of him. That's the beginning of empathy. And in that moment the lie that the world is divided into good guys and bad guys comes crashing down. And in that moment I hope people will think about the many, many ways in which we are all closer to the perpetrators than we like to think." Turning Congo into a menacing "other," with no connections to our selves, is a fraud that Oppenheimer works hard not to let viewers get away with.

But putting this empathy into practice during the production was grueling for Oppenheimer nonetheless. "My biggest challenge on the film was coping emotionally, being so close to this horror for so long and trying not to become numb or hateful. You know, empathy is not a zero sum game. I don't think if you empathize with Anwar that you have any less empathy for others." Carrying this philosophy into the moral mazes that hounded him every day would keep him up, literally, both day and night. It was a daunting goal, but he held fast to it as hard as he could, even when it left him isolated and morally ravaged. "Empathy is the beginning of love, and I don't think you can have too much of it."

Oppenheimer is keenly aware that an all-consuming film like *The Act of Killing* won't be one he can sock away and easily move forward from. The film's story will likely swim parallel to his own for many years to come. Even after its release, phantasmagorical bits of the tale continue to emerge. There's one that still blows Oppenheimer away.

One of Anwar Congo's favorite songs, as it happens, is Peggy Lee's mournful classic, "Is That All There Is?" To Congo, says Oppenheimer, the song sums up his failure to reach the heights of power and influence that some of his contemporaries achieved. One day the two were driving around the mountains of north Sumatra looking for a suitable location to film a scene around "Is That All There Is?" Coming around a bend, Oppenheimer lurched the car to a stop when he saw in front of them a massive, four-story high, brightly-painted concrete goldfish.

What was this giant fish doing here? Congo told him that the fish was a sad story, because it had been a popular seafood restaurant for many years, but had closed and was now just a shell of its glory days. Oppenheimer knew their search was over: "It's a perfect location for 'Is That All There Is?' because it was a beautiful place, had been looted over the years, and now it's so disappointing what's become of it. It's this artifact of human fantasy that just doesn't go away." Oppenheimer was riveted by the fish and would film a chilling and highly memorable musical number there, complete with giddy dancers at the fish's mouth and a roaring thunderstorm behind them. He even uses a still from the scene for the movie's publicity posters.

But what he didn't know about the fish setting at the time, but which he believes may partly explain his fascination with it, is something he would find out only after the film was complete. It turns out that just behind the fish lies the notorious Lake Toba, a vast crater that is believed to be the site of a massive supervolcano that erupted about 75,000 years ago. It caused a volcanic winter that killed nearly every single human on earth. Scientists call it the Toba Super Catastrophe.

To the director, the juxtaposition of the deadly lake and Congo's dance number is uncanny. It represents no less than "the poetic truth of what the whole film is about, a film about how we get lost in the fantasy, the seductive stories we tell, and the dreams we conjure despite the disaster, the onrushing apocalypse" heading straight for us. Oppenheimer's remarkable film brings viewers right into Congo and company's giddy conga line, dancing at the abyss.

Postscript: For his work on The Act Of Killing, Oppenheimer would in September 2014 be awarded a highly prestigious MacArthur Foundation "Genius Grant." He will receive a no-strings-attached stipend of $625,000 spread out over 5 years.

7

GasLand

DIRECTOR AND PRODUCER
Josh Fox

Oscar Nominee, Best Documentary Feature—2010

SUMMARY
Josh Fox's brash and brazen road trip through an America landscape besieged by what Fox calls an all-out assault from the oil and gas fracking industry. Personal, touching, and at times shocking, Fox's debut doc gem quickly became part of the national conversation about the controversial practice of fracking.

During much of Josh Fox's 25-year career as a theater director, he'd leaned on the documentary approach to his work—interview real life people in sundry personal and political dilemmas and then gently fictionalize those accounts for the stage.

But when Fox first grew alarmed about the controversial energy extraction process known as "fracking," (hydraulic fracturing) he felt in his bones it may be time to ditch the fictionalizing part.

In 2009, he started hearing mysterious tales from the fracking front lines all around his Milanville, Pennsylvania home—of ink black water in neighbors' bathtubs; disfigured pets; of water supplies so polluted by fracking chemicals that residents could light their tap water on fire; and about backyard well explosions.

Hydraulic fracturing is the process of extracting oil and natural gas from deep, underground shale deposits by injecting water mixed with sand and chemicals at high pressures. The injection fractures rocks, and loosens up oil and gas deposits, which can then be extracted. Proponents rave about its nearly endless potential as an energy source, while critics complain it ravages the environment, is a chemical assault against public health and the landscape and can cause earthquakes.

When Fox started talking to his neighbors about how fracking had impacted their lives, he grew increasingly alarmed. Moved by these stories, he got in his car and began to drive around the towns he'd known since childhood in the northeast corner of Pennsylvania. "This idea of water being lit on fire, it was just, like 'I have to see that.' It was like a fire in my brain. I had to go find and see that," he recalls.

He didn't yet know if these stories had any truth to them. And one after the other, randomly chosen residents confirmed the horror stories. All of a sudden, "even though it was happening 8,000 feet underground, it all became real to me."

Professionally, the timing was perfect for a break. His theater company had just finished a series of major projects, and he had some down time to figure out which projects to take on next. Neighbors' stories were filling Fox's head—outrageously fouled water, unexplained bronchial maladies, and unscrupulous out-of-state energy executives criss-crossing nearby farms with checkbooks in hand. He found himself "sucked in ... It was like, 'Am I gonna do this? Can I do this?'" Quickly, his fears turned into what he describes as "a calling," and that calling would eventually turn into the superb *GasLand*, nominated for Best Documentary Feature Oscar and a trusty fuse ever since for igniting anti-fracking sentiment around the world.

GasLand is enormously watchable, and a startling doc debut. It's pacey, low-fi, off kilter and very often funny. The film is the inquisitive, impassioned and (slightly) angry voice of everyman Fox, the banjo-strumming narrator and guide through a country he thought he knew. The film is a quest in the truest sense—constantly asking questions that yield more deception than consolation. It's scrappy, singular, and deeply personal.

Once word got out in his community that Fox was planning to travel around and gather peoples' fracking stories on camera, the public reached out to him, beseeching him to come hear their tales. "Can you come here? Can you go there? Can you come to this other place? ... " Casting was underway before he even knew it.

Next, he needed some funding to be able to hit the road. He'd travel mostly alone, sleep in his car or in people's homes, and eat as he could. Laying out his plan to friends and relatives, he soon gathered up $2,500 in donations— enough for the very basics.

A powerful image floated in his head as he began planning for his shoot. Stuck in his head, motivating his quest, was the image of Wyoming ... a place whose stark beauty hit him early and hard. "When I was 21 or 22 years old, I had traveled across Wyoming one summer and completely fell in love with the state, criss-crossed it, and went to every mountain range and weird prairie ... " But in researching fracking for the film he hoped to make, he could barely recognize the place. Whole stretches of the state, given over to fracking, had turned into apocalyptic "moonscapes." He committed himself to trying to keep his besieged patch of northeastern Pennsylvania, and every other part of the country, from that same fate.

So, in the Spring of 2009, he finds himself with enough money to scrape together a shoot, enthusiastic backers, and a burning need to tell the story. What he lacks is any knowledge at all about how to make a documentary film. To pull that off, he'd have to do what he'd encouraged his theater actors to do for years—be confident, focused, and improvise well.

His previous shooting experience was patchy—filming some of his staged shows and a low-budget feature film called *Memorial Day* (2008). Oddly, both

his shooting for the stage and the feature took place entirely at night. Until *GasLand*, he had never shot in the daytime before.

But he credits his stage background with helping him conquer the steep learning curve. "Having an aesthetic sense already, whether it's onstage, writing, or in music, if you pick up a different kind of instrument, in this case a camera, it's not like your aesthetic mind disappears." And *GasLand*'s style reflects that loose ethos—at times starkly beautiful and solemn, and often rambling, unsteady and jumpy. Some viewers might feel a little seasick at times, as the camera occasionally lunges through scenes, lingering here and then zipping over to there.

"You experiment. I have a sense of what I want to see, what kind of style … But I want people to know that (my shooting) is all self-taught." Fox mostly discards with a tripod, shoots himself at awkward angles while walking around and while driving, and captures lots of sonic noise in his mics. Some might scoff, but many of the film's fans find the rambling style a vital source of its energy and drive, and a hallmark of Fox's fresh-faced search for answers to his questions about fracking. He believes that a slickly packaged visual look can feel "alienating, too perfect." In fact, he's proud to assert, "the whole *GasLand* aesthetic is the reaction to what people think of as 'beautiful.'"

So, unencumbered by much of conventional wisdom about the documentary craft, he sets out in Spring 2009 to make a film focusing, at first, on his nearby area. His aims, initially, are modest: help illuminate for his neighbors the looming underground dangers in their backyards.

Considering the global phenomenon that *GasLand* would become barely a year later, it's striking how small scale it sounds as Fox describes how it first took shape. "It was very, very local, and all we wanted was to supply objective information from a person in the area about the subject."

As Fox describes it, it was a decision that wasn't even in his hands. "When you're inspired to do a project, something weird just says, this is your job, you have to do this. It doesn't matter that any rational person would say this isn't your job. Clearly you have to talk about this."

So he traveled around his patch of Pennsylvania, keying especially on the area around the nearby town of Dimock, a hotbed of fracking activity. "When the crisis came to my backyard, it was clear that this was going to be a huge transformative moment in the history of that area, which I had known for 40 years." He harvested ever more worrying tales, and then set out to edit a short film, hoping to raise the alarm about what he saw as a region under virtual attack.

Post-Production was a ramshackle process. Fox and partners cobbled together pieces of various lengths as soon as he got home from shoots ("a ten-minute segment here, a 15-minute segments there"), and then screened them, right away, to anybody who wanted to watch.

Initial audiences were intrigued enough that the theater director in him took over and Fox began to cook up more provocative ways to screen the film. He settled on a colorful plan: drive a truck up to the banks of the Delaware River and screen the scenes from the back of the truck for anybody around. No charge, and Fox and partners would lead Q&A sessions afterward. Small but enthusiastic audiences were enthralled, and more kept coming. Fox realized he'd struck a nerve. "We rapidly figured out that it was a debate that was much bigger than just my backyard, just my area ... and that this would affect millions of people."

So, a fantasy he'd toyed with early on began to take shape as something that he might be able to pull off: turn this material into a feature film. The questions and worries of the "focus groups" gathered along the Delaware for the truck-side screenings persuaded him he had to try to expand his vision nationally.

"The thought that this place, the Upper Delaware River Basin, which is such a treasure, could get destroyed by the oil and gas industry was a nightmare scenario and was hanging over my head. I couldn't sleep. It was nerve wracking. The idea just started to gain momentum ... "

The riverside screening audiences not only pushed him to expand, but they also gave him crucial feedback that would prove invaluable later. For one thing, Fox noticed that audiences seemed to connect better with the material when he was on camera rather than just off-camera narrating, or not part of the scene at all.

"As a director, I didn't really want to be in the movie. I didn't want to be in the center of the focus. But people responded to the humor of the film, the narration, the tone, to the way they were guided through that experience… So we decided we were gonna keep it," he recalls.

Buoyed by the screenings, Fox began to burn with the need to find out how the rest of the country was faring against the onslaught of fracking. Put simply, "we wanted to become part of the national dialogue." Was tiny Dimock PA an outlier, or was it a bitter glimpse of a national dystopia? Though a complete doc novice, and guided largely by trial and error, Fox had an advantage few others enjoy—he'd screened an extended "trailer" for several hundred people already, and had taken careful mental notes on what worked—and what fell flat.

But would an expanded *GasLand* play in Peoria? Did anyone else care? Frankly, Fox didn't even care. He just knew he had to get started. "I had a suspicion that what we had going was going to make some waves," he admits. So, it was back to the '92 Camry to hit the road again, farther afield, to see what he could see.

It was one thing to interview residents about the toll fracking was taking on their families' lives. But Fox knew that to really tell the full fracking picture, to create a full-bodied film about the whole industry, that he needed to see the other side as well—those in the fracking industry who made millions while so many residents suffered.

For after all, fracking typically involved the consent of people whose farms and yards were thought to sit atop shale deposits. The industry deployed an army of friendly, loquacious, and low-key foot soldiers to walk through neighborhoods and fields and entice people to accept payments in exchange for allowing fracking on their land. Of course, the effects of fracking could ripple outwards under rock and the water table for miles, and harm people in a wide radius. But at its core, and though many would later come to regret it, many Americans were saying yes to the payments, and inviting industry to drill fracking wells on their land.

As Fox describes it, "the gas industry was going out, waving around all this money, and talking about how it was environmentally friendly and there were no problems and nothing was going to change…" But Fox met many people whose suffering was compounded by wracking guilt: they'd damaged or even destroyed their families' health for a few dollars.

Having made the decision to appear on screen in the film, Fox would have to constantly wrestle with just how much to appear, and in what types of settings. "I just ask people lots of questions, questions audiences have to answer for themselves, in a way that tries not to get in the way of the subject itself. I was very conscious of making sure that I was doing as little as possible as a narrator, and in the frame as little as possible so as to highlight the real storytellers in the film."

But whether he likes it or not, Fox's presence in the film keeps the journey and the questing moving amiably forward. When he's not on screen, we find ourselves in a more conventional, journalism-based and idea-driven doc. When he comes back on, we feel anchored once again to his hunt for answers. His affable, gee-whiz manner is infectious, and he refrains from ever wanting to "gotcha" his subjects.

At one point, Fox walks into a conference room to interview a representative from the Colorado Oil and Gas Conservation Commission. Fox had gone into the interview believing that the subject represents "a corrupt agency. They shield the oil and gas industry, and don't stand up for their constituents." Fox wants to hear his side of the debate, but before they have even really begun to talk, the representative walks out on him. Some viewers may want to lunge after the man, shake him, make him stay, make him account for himself. But this is not Fox's style. After the walkout, Fox lingers in the room, jaws agape, hanging. At times like these some may wish Fox had a little more bile in his blood. On the other hand, Fox's resignation may be the only honest way to approach that situation. Drawing intimate, candid material from people on camera is a process that Fox likens to a "friendship," where the filmmaker deploys a "compassionate lens." He sums up his non-confrontational approach this way: "Respect people's humanity, as you're moving toward getting information."

Fox points to another testy moment in the film when he is interviewing John Hanger, head of the Department of Environmental Protection in Pennsylvania. Hanger is uncomfortable and tentative and clearly has some degree of sympathy with the victims of fracking in his state, but also feels compelled to maintain political composure in the face of Fox's roll call of ills felling Hanger's constituents. At one point, Fox asks Hanger if he'd be willing to drink some of the tap water he's brought back from a farm with fracking wells. Hanger demurs. "(My approach) was very different than slamming down the bottle on the table: 'Drink it!' It was a 'mild ask,'" Fox explains, summing up his preferred approach to those kinds of adversarial encounters.

Fox's singular presence on camera emerges not just from his naturally bewildered face, but also with his banjo. At random points in the film, Fox, wearing a gas mask and looking straight into the camera, will get out his banjo and simply knock out a short tune. He also uses the charming and quirky instrument as a fail-safe ice-breaker with some of the characters he meets. In one particularly inspired lick, Fox knocks out "This Land Is Your Land", a poignant love song to a beautiful country, but one that he sees as ripped apart by greed. "That (song) was particularly ironic ... It just happened naturally. Going out to that (fracking) site and feeling like I needed to do that there. You try a lot of stuff. You never know what's going to hit."

Fox cites the late banjo god emeritus and water activist Pete Seeger as the inspiration for this piece of musical theater. As random as they are riveting, Fox uses the musical interludes as punctuation marks, playing havoc with linear form while underscoring the sense of sci-fi weirdness, and looming apocalypse that hangs over America while it's getting fracked.

Fox experiments further with some innovative camera techniques. Mostly eschewing a tripod, the camera sometimes whip pans around a room. Frequent shots of fracking sites taken from the moving car (including some that appear to be shot by the driver) give a disorienting feel and pace. When Fox and his editor, Matt Sanchez, had a scene whose content they liked but where the shooting was poor, they would project it onto a wall and shoot it off the wall. They sometimes did this to turn a 4×3 shot into High Definition.

Likewise with TV news clips. They had access to numerous high quality clips from affiliates. But they didn't sit well with Fox. "It's too clear. It puts you into that semi-somnabulistic state you get watching TV, and we didn't want that." So Fox opted to grunge it up a bit by playing those clips on his computer, and then shooting them off the computer. And whenever they wanted to speed up, and dirty up, a scene, they'd do the same—shoot it on a computer, sped up. Techniques both creative and unusual, and cheaper work-arounds for achieving the results Fox and Sanchez were after.

The whole visual conceit of *GasLand* "trends toward the verite, personal camera style," explains Fox. "It's grittier, but I think capable of more serenity and more beauty because it's so personal."

You could even argue that Fox needed to deploy a ragtag bag of camera tricks as he did, since so much of the film's engine is fueled by such a simple and straightforward theme—betrayal. We meet a parade of well-meaning people, across America, who made the mistake of trusting oil and gas reps who lied to them, and destroyed their families and their livelihoods. That is the heart of the film. "You watch that kindness manifest over and over again, and then you watch it betrayed. That's what's so upsetting," says Fox.

Formally, and structurally, the setups are repetitive. But that doesn't mean that viewers will be gritting their teeth in anger any less after the 10th such encounter, than at the first.

The smorgasbord of ailments Fox's characters blame on fracking is staggering: dizziness, hair and sensory loss, constant headaches and nausea, sever bone aches, neuropathy. Fox was the primary shooter, but the days were often so long, and the stories so riveting, that he called on numerous friends to help him cover more ground wherever he traveled.

The film portrays places we think we have something of a handle on—the Great Plains, suburban Texas—and inverts them, via the lens of fracking. Fracking wells and equipment seem to have devoured the landscape Fox captures. Secrets and lies about fracking govern interactions between the public, corporations and the government. Residents complain of multiple ailments, and people they trust tell them their symptoms are a mirage. One woman finds herself, against her better judgment, keeping in her freezer a menagerie of dead animals killed by a polluted creek. "It's creepy, it's not normal, it's unnatural," she admits, with evident alarm.

In Fox's topsy-turvy world, sometimes humor is the only way to stay sane. As when he sees ribbons of gaily colored ribbons draped over a toxic wastewater pit. "Colored flags?" he asks, deadpan. "I have no idea what those are for. The grand opening of a new pit?"

And there are loopy digressions aplenty, including Fox bouncing like a toddler on an oversize brown couch that he assures us is without a doubt "the most comfortable couch in America." At one point Fox plays out the emotions of many viewers when he simply can't take it anymore. A polluted creek reminds him of one near his Pennsylvania home and, on camera, he comes apart and begins weeping. At another point, in a kind of coda, Fox confesses that "I wanted to get out of GasLand, but there was nowhere to go."

The "everything and the kitchen sink" flavor to the editing is a hallmark of Fox's working style. Impulsive, restless, punchy. And for a novice, he manages to pull off a raw and rangy road trip of the most thankless kind. The Post schedule, bankrolled by about $11,000 they brought in from fund-raising parties, started in May 2009, and was a decidedly catch as catch can affair. Fox and editor Matt Sanchez edited as and when they could, at night, by day, and in between real jobs like Fox's ongoing theater commitments. Cutting in parallel, as it were, they'd bring each other scenes as they were ready, exchange comments, and then go back for more.

That November 2009, they sent what they had—a 2-1/2 half hour "mess" as Fox describes it—to Sundance. Sundance showed some interest, and they then quickly sent them some more and shorter cuts. To their astonishment, Sundance sent them a grant for $20,000 to beef up their audio. They put the grant to use and then got offered a spot in the festival.

But, Fox's production being the obsessive quest it had always been, they kept on editing all the way up until the following January, 2010, when it finally screened in Utah. Once they got accepted into Sundance, the phone had rung pretty much off the hook but to no avail. "I wasn't finished with the film, so I really didn't want to pick up the phone. … I didn't even know what a sales agent was," admits Fox.

On top of that, Fox was also opening a major play in New York at the exact same time, in January. 30 cast members needed his guidance, and in Utah they needed his film. Yesterday. "Chaos. I was shuttling back and forth between the play and the sound mix. Basically didn't sleep for three weeks."

An HBO executive brought into the Sundance screening was smitten, and she sent it to her boss, the estimable head of HBO documentaries, Sheila Nevins. Nevins loved it too, the film won a Special Jury Prize at Sundance, and HBO offered Fox a TV deal. This fit into Fox's plans perfectly, because he wasn't ready to give up the theatrical rights. With funds coming in for the TV sale, Fox once again hit the road, but this time with a polished, Sundance-winning film. Adulation poured in even more after *GasLand* was nominated in 2011 for an Oscar for Best Feature Documentary. Fox and his team have shown it to hundreds of thousands of people across the United States and the world, and he and his team continue to screen it. Popular demand drew Fox to make a sequel, *GasLand 2*, which is also in fast motion on the festival circuit, and in schools and conferences worldwide.

What does the future hold for Fox? "I think we're done making GasLand films. I'm definitely moving on," he says, eager for the next chapter. He'll continue to promote and screen the two *GasLand* films, but is looking beyond. "*GasLand* is a movie about how we are being sold to the highest bidder. It's a movie about power. These are themes that can take me, as a filmmaker, in a million different directions ... ."

8

Undefeated

DIRECTOR AND PRODUCER
Daniel Lindsay

DIRECTOR
T.J. Martin

Oscar Winner, Best Documentary Feature—2011

SUMMARY
Undefeated *looks at the players and the drama in the 2009 football season of the beleaguered Manassas Tigers of Memphis—a perennial doormat African-American squad led by a mesmerizing white coach known as Big Daddy Snowflake.*

The jump from Beer Pong to Oscar was surprisingly swift for T.J. Martin and Daniel Lindsay. One minute (2007), making what their bosses hoped would be a simple "grope fest" about "drunk dudes throwing up on each other," and in the next (2009) hard at work on an Oscar winner. Such is the delicious good fortune of Messrs. Martin and Lindsay.

At the time they get hired in 2007 by Film 101, the production company behind *Last Cup: Road to the World Series of Beer Pong*, both Martin and Lindsay are restless. Creatively, they're hungry but in a rut. Martin is creating background visuals for Top 40 musical acts like Madonna and is "just sick of it. It was soulless." Lindsay is working on some sketch comedy gigs, and he too is eager to work on a "real doc."

Beer Pong becomes the glue that bonds them. Lindsay directs, and Martin cuts it. Their work on the surprisingly thoughtful film makes them realize "we have a similar work ethic, which is a really unhealthy one," says Martin. Workaholism, that is.

The two realize they can easily just poke fun at the downwardly mobile slackers who populate the Beer Pong universe. At first, they don't care about that world in the least. They just want to make a documentary. Almost any one.

But to their surprise, they're drawn in, smitten. "We really fell in love with our characters and took a really earnest approach to the material." A planned 3-month edit stretches out to 9 months, and the two end up profiling "four guys having this existential crisis, but set against a beer pong tournament." Their high-concept take on a lowbrow subject becomes a surprise semi-hit, lures Morgan Spurlock aboard as Executive Producer, and cements their professional partnership. "Dan and I really just fell in love with each other's process from there, and decided to start working together."

As Post on that film winds down, they begin scouting around for good material for a documentary, something all their own, that will let them cut loose from working around the edges of the Hollywood content mill. They're in their late 20s, and eager to jump quickly onto a strong story that excites their curiosity. If it pays some bills, so much the better.

Early in 2009, a producer friend named Rich Middlemas sends the two an article he digs out of the Memphis Commercial Appeal that he thought they'd be interested in. "Have you read 'The Blind Side?'," he asks them. "It's kind of happening again." They weren't familiar with the book. The title, by Michael Lewis, had come out in 2006 (W.W. Norton). It's a story about strife and maternal bonds between the wife of a high-school football coach and one of his star players. The article that Middlemas sent to Lindsay and Martin happened to tell a similar story.

The Appeal article looked at a troubled but stellar Manassas High tackle named OC Brown, who was living part time with his coach in a mansion in a posh white Memphis suburb and part time with his grandmother in a crime-ridden neighborhood near his school. They were fascinated by OC Brown's story and wanted to see if they could turn the tale into a compelling film.

So in late March 2009, producer Middlemas and Lindsay get on a plane to Memphis to find out. They'd spend a week scouting characters and locations, come back, powwow with TJ, and decide if there is anything there. But what they discover in Memphis takes them by surprise. OC Brown indeed turns out to be a great character. But he has lots of company—other fascinating personalities on the team too who the filmmakers hadn't even considered, notably sensitive and brilliant linebacker Montrail "Money" Brown; and the angry, sullen but mesmerizing lineman, Chavis Daniels.

And one of the most intriguing characters of all was one who wasn't high on their radar—the flamboyant, monster personality coach of the team, Bill Courtney. He'd picked up the filmmakers at the airport when they arrived, and they got to interview him on their last day of the scout.

"We met Bill and he told us the history of the team and everything, and that was when we decided to shift the focus and use the season as a frame to tell the story and open up their world," says Lindsay. They would focus on OC Brown, some of his teammates, and Coach Bill, and drape all of these characters across the football season as their dramatic through line.

This plan gets them over a hurdle they faced with their original OC Brown-driven concept of the film: much of that story is well underway. But by turning toward the football season and toward team-coach dynamics, they can make the vérité style, forward-moving film that is more in their comfort zone.

As coach Courtney relays it, the Manassas Tigers football squad is a 110-year-long tragedy—zero playoff victories since 1899; appalling coaches;

players in and out of prison or killed; empty stands and emptier coffers; and the shame of a school itself considered a basket case.

By the time Courtney, a local lumberman, came on as a volunteer in 2003, they had won just 5 games in the previous decade and fielded only 17 players—far fewer than even Pop Warner teams in the tony stretches of Memphis where Courtney lived. In fact, Manassas was reduced to the ultimate in football whoredom—selling "pay games," whereby teams would pay for the privilege of beating the pulp out of Manassas. It was the team's chief source of funds.

But some recent buzz in the college football scout world about OC Brown, and praise for Coach Bill's program, makes Martin and Lindsay think that the Tigers' 2009 season might be less bleak than the previous century's. So, on a second scout trip in the Spring of 2009, they shoot nearly non-stop, hoping to harvest great material from both the on- and off-field lives of the players.

There is one scene in particular that Middlemas and Lindsay shot on the scout that blows Martin away. It's the kind of scene you can't plan but simply unfolds quietly and potently. This one involves a small turtle and stands out as one of the film's ineffable moments.

"One of the first things that Dan shot with Money was the turtle scene. Money says that 'turtles are like people—they've gotta be hard on the outside, but soft on the inside.' I sat there and I watched it and thought 'That's the scene!' Who says stuff like that? To stumble upon a community that was so open already .... we have to move there and just embed ourselves and we'll continue to get more stuff like that!"

During the scout trips, Martin stays back home in LA cutting together small scenes and showing them around in hopes of getting some backing. He's helped by two veteran documentary makers who had offered themselves as Producers—Seth Gordon and ex-NFL player Ed Cunningham, the duo behind the quirky and celebrated documentary *The King of Kong: A Fistful of*

Quarters. They give Martin and Lindsay vital support from the very beginning and urge them to stay with the quickly unfolding story.

And so they do. In July 2009, the two up and move from LA to Memphis, bent on making themselves both omnipresent and invisible in the world of Manassas High and its remarkable football team for at least the next 9 months. They start shooting as soon as they get there, in time for pre-season training and the fall football season.

While the duo are still shooting, *The Blind Side* movie, starring Sandra Bullock, is released into theaters. Despite some similar plot lines, Martin and Lindsay basically ignore the feature, focusing on their own documentary.

"I think we used The Blind Side movie mostly as a cautionary tale," explains Lindsay. "We looked at how they treated that relationship (between the black football player and Sandra Bullock's surrogate mother), and I think it was somewhat irresponsible ... We were very cautious of telling a 'white knight' story. It's something we didn't want to do."

To them, a nuanced approach to the story's racial themes and class dynamics comes naturally. They won't play up the film's obvious socio-economic differences to help "sell" the narrative. Lindsay: "When we went into it we thought, 'Oh, maybe there's going to be an interesting dynamic between him and the kids,' but so quickly you realize the kids didn't care that he was white and he didn't either."

By the time they start shooting in July 2009, all they have is a tentative okay from Coach Bill and some of the players. But how can two hipster outsiders (Martin hails from Seattle and Lindsay from northern Illinois), trundling camera gear from their Hollywood homes, hope to fit in with the virtually all black, hardscrabble world of Manassas? How can they gain the trust and confidence they crave, to get the 24/7 access they need?

Their solution? "Just being around, all the time," says Lindsay. "On our initial trips from California I'm sure they thought, 'Oh, we'll never see those guys again.' And then we did, and then we moved there!"

Securing Coach Bill's support was essential.

"Bill did kind of sit the whole team down and say, 'You know, I've felt these guys out, and they're here to tell your story. If I didn't think their intentions were good, I wouldn't let them around you.' So we ended up becoming like an extension of the team."

But just a week into the school year they get some bad news: "We got a call from the principal when we were about to leave to shoot at school one day, and she said: 'You guys aren't allowed to come back here anymore.'" The School District is shutting them down. District officials hear there is a film crew working on campus, claims they aren't properly permitted, and tell them to please go back to Hollywood.

"It was basically, 'Get those guys out of here.' ... We had to try to re-convince them to let us in," says Lindsay.

The District had been battered in recent years by intensely negative local news coverage of their bedraggled schools, and they were sick of all media coverage.

But the timing to get shut down couldn't be worse. The Tigers got blown out in the first game of the season, and a crucial second game is coming up. That Friday night Martin and Lindsay have to watch only but not shoot, as the Tigers pull off a stunning upset to win in the closing seconds.

To try to get the school board's okay, they realize they'll have to do something they vowed they'd never do: show anyone not on their production team footage while they're shooting.

"We didn't want to show anybody our approach. You open up a can of worms that way," says Lindsay. But their backs are against the wall and they have no choice. The whole film is in jeopardy. With the help of Coach Bill, once again, they get a meeting with District officials, and show her a 6-minute reel. A "no" vote, and the film is in peril. Martin and Lindsay are on pins and needles when they start playing the reel.

"We wanted it to pull at the heart strings, to give us leverage," Martin recalls.

Then, part way through the screening, Lindsay notices a smile spreading on the face of a school district lawyer in the room. "She got very emotional watching it. She was like, 'That's the neighborhood I grew up in. That's what it looks like. That's what it feels like ... ' So then they were, 'Okay, you guys are good to go again. We'll sign this.'" To cement the deal, the filmmakers also decide to offer the school district a portion of any profits the film might make—something that seems nearly impossible to any of them at that point.

Now with Coach Bill, the team, and the school district on board, they just have to find a way to shoot a whole season's worth of football games, and to stitch them into a coherent film.

"We wanted to make a verite film that played like a narrative. The only way to do it was to get ourselves on the team, and then just kind of shoot everything," says Martin. But to do this, they'd have to overcome a key paradox. As Lindsay discovers, "high school football is really boring to watch, but it's very exciting for the people that are in it."

The duo also very consciously resist making yet another triumphant underdog sports story, so familiar to Americans and—to Martin and Lindsay —so full of clichés.

"We fought the (traditional) football story for a long time, but once we saw it, the season itself was turning out to be something pretty special. By game 5," it was a different story, Martin recalls. "We realized, we better just make the best damn football movie we can make."

All along, in order to get maximum access and candor, Martin and Lindsay made themselves into as lean a crew as they could, with just the two of them shooting, capturing sound straight into the camera, and using no sound mixers or boom operators.

To that point, Martin and Lindsay had mostly edited or directed. For this film they decide they'd continue these roles—but to do all the shooting themselves as well. Occasionally, they would add extra shooters to cover more material during games or wide shots in the crowd. At one point, they also need to bring on some extra help when Martin breaks his hand shooting. But basically, it's just them. Though far less experienced than many shooters they could have hired, Martin crosses his fingers and hopes that "because of the film's emotional content, you forget how little the budget was and you're forgiving the camera mistakes, forgiving everything!"

To try blend in as easily as they could, they also go as low-tech as possible—using cheap, solid state cameras and crummy-looking gear. "We just looked like we were college students running around making a little project. It was disarming for people," says Martin. So disarming, in fact, that sometimes Manassas students don't even know filming is underway. "Who's going to play me in the movie?" students would ask the filmmakers. "No, this *is* the movie. We're filming. *You're* going to play you!"

Though they never planned on being the film's primary shooters, they say that the pressure of shooting forced them to improve—quickly. Lindsay: "I tried really hard to be an active listener ... What I learned about my own shooting was that my ability to listen, and listen with the camera, was like giving the audience a point of view."

They shoot from July till almost Christmas, non-stop, ending up with a walloping 500+ hours of footage to sort through. Not just football games, but practically every school assembly, show, after-school club and—it seems—nearly every hallway gossip session—too, along with endless hours of time with players at home. It's all there, ready to swallow up their lives all over again in Post.

After a 2-week break, they come back to Memphis in January 2010 to log and cut scenes and end up staying until April. They go to Memphis both to reduce home distractions and to be able to grab any pick-up shots they might need during Post.

Structurally, they decide to place the football season as the central narrative train and then to weave off-field, personal stories of the players in and out of the main story spine. They agree on that quickly.

But while Production was stressful and full-on, as it usually is, Post would present new challenges. Could the two work just feet apart staring at hours and hours of footage and come to agreeable solutions, without too much stress?

"When we're talking (in Post), it can look like we're mad at each other. And if we know something's not working but we can't figure it out, we'll take it out on each other," concedes Lindsay. "But we're never really getting mad. We're not really yelling. That's just the way we communicate."

Martin says that, ultimately, "we want the same outcome," and that's what saved them. They agree to hit hard on the theme of fatherhood. Coach Bill, abandoned by his father as a young boy, becoming a strong father figure to the Manassas team—many of them also fatherless.

Certain lines and scenes resonate strongly with both of them: in the scene where Money begins sobbing after he's told that a donor is giving him a free ride through college, Lindsay finds himself breaking down too in the edit room. That scene's in. Coach Bill's bombastic: "You think football builds character? Football REVEALS character!" The screen practically shakes during the delivery. No question there between Lindsay and Martin—that makes the cut.

Martin also says neither of them is "precious with their ideas, or defensive." So, the process may appear messy and taut, but for them, it works. And they hope to continue their partnership for as long as they can.

They go back to LA in April to begin the real story-building and cut the film over the next 10 months. Finally, by February 2011, they feel like they have something they can show the rest of the world.

Undefeated is accepted to South By Southwest in Austin in March that year, and that will be their unveiling. Even a couple of years later, Martin still shakes his head and seems baffled by what went down in Austin. "Totally random and surreal is the only way to describe it."

The day of their Sunday night screening, a number of heavies ask to see screeners. William Morris Endeavour was their sales agent, and Paramount,

Disney, and others had asked for a look. Then on Monday morning, perhaps also feeling some "buzz" around the film, Harvey Weinstein asks to see it.

They spend a fitful day in Austin, and then at a reception just before the screening, a man walks up to Martin and Lindsay. "Hi, I'm David Glasser from The Weinstein Company. I'm here to buy your film."

"It was just wild," Martin recalls. "We didn't expect anything like that."

The screening plays to rapturous applause. Most of the cast is there, and afterwards they all go out and celebrate. "We get a phone call at like 8 in the morning at our hotel room, and it was one of our producers who said 'You guys all in the room? Congratulations. There was a bidding war all night for your film...'"

The Weinsteins win the bidding war, and the deal is now officially done. A reputed seven figures for distribution and remake rights. Released later that year, the film gets a 96 percent "Certified Fresh" rating on Rotten Tomatoes, stellar reviews, and wide theatrical release.

Then, on January 21, 2012, Martin and Lindsay get another shocking early morning phone call. The Academy of Motion Picture Arts & Sciences picks them for an Oscar nomination. More stardust follows right after the Oscar nomination when Sean "P. Diddy" Combs calls to talk about the film.

Combs tells an interviewer the film had him "crying like a baby." Combs meets with the filmmakers and tells them "about how he played high school football and about how his coach turned his back on him after he got hurt, and how much that pained him."

Combs signs on as an Executive Producer and gives them the keys to the public relations machinery of P. Diddy Inc. So while the filmmakers score big with gushy interviews on the likes of NPR and CNN, Combs takes them into another realm—chatting up the film on talk shows like Jimmy Kimmel and Ellen DeGeneres.

February 26, 2012— the icing on the cake. Martin and Lindsay win the Oscar for Best Documentary Feature, making Martin the first African-American to ever win in that category. In his excitement, Martin drops an unfortunate "F-Bomb" in his acceptance speech but later apologizes.

To Dan Lindsay, the Oscar is a mixed blessing—both a wonder and a curse. "It's a blessing because of the perceived notion of what that means, more opportunities open up to you. It's a curse because suddenly there's an expectation that you have to be able to repeat what you just did."

Lindsay says the statuette maintains a place of pride in a cupboard "next to the Scotch bottles" and occasionally friends will come over and ask to take their picture with it. But mostly it just sits there, haunting and fascinating him. "I still have trouble understanding it because it just doesn't make any sense to me."

For Martin and Lindsay, as with most Oscar winners, the "Oscar bounce" lasts only so long and then it's back to work. They want to continue to work together. Documentary projects are offered. Narrative scripts sit in the in-box. Ears open and still young, they're eager to explore what comes their way.

Reflecting on the struggles making *Undefeated*, Lindsay could be speaking for many documentary makers when he says: "The amount of problems we had is also in some ways almost equal to the amount of luck we had in making this film."

After all the anxieties in pushing *Undefeated* forward, the high drama of the Tigers season nearly matching the high stakes for the two, Lindsay heard a single review that meant more to them than all the Oscar and box office accolades.

"After our subjects watched the film, they told us 'You got it right.' And that was the most … that was the biggest reward in making the movie, because they trusted us so much to do it, for them to actually say that we got it right."

9

Restrepo

DIRECTORS AND PRODUCERS
Sebastian Junger and Tim Hetherington

Oscar Nomination, Best Documentary Feature, 2010

SUMMARY
*An inside look at American combat troops in a notoriously
dangerous valley in Afghanistan.*

Sebastian Junger is a hard-bitten combat journalist who created one of the great chronicles of modern warfare in *Restrepo*, his nail-biting documentary debut set in a notoriously deadly valley deep in Afghanistan. And like so many of his fellow wartime filmmakers, he several times nearly paid the ultimate price for his work—in a series of deadly, close-range firefights that he caught on camera.

Junger's co-director, Tim Hetherington, also survived the fighting in Afghanistan, but then was killed in April 2011, less than a year after the film was released. The British-American photographer and war correspondent was bombed while covering the uprising in Libya. Hetherington's death, in circumstances still unclear, stunned the world and so aggrieved Junger that he swore off war reporting forever. He was supposed to be with Hetherington in Libya but had canceled his flight at the last minute.

So *Restrepo* stands as a riveting snapshot of war as seen through the eyes of a duo who will never give us the same view again. With stunning intimacy and candor, the soldiers of Second Platoon, B Company, 2nd Battalion, 503rd Infantry Regiment (airborne), 173rd Airborne Brigade Combat Team fight fear, bullets, boredom, anxiety, and—on occasion—each other, for months on end. Bunkered down in Camp Restrepo (named after a fallen comrade) on a stark Korengal Valley outcropping, the men look like sitting ducks in the enemy-infested landscape. Their weapons may be state-of-the-art, but their mission seems a jumbled, contradictory, and unworkable mess. In a series of sometimes excruciating meetings with local village elders, the soldiers try in vain to pull local sentiment to their side. But viewers can see how futile the exchanges are: the US Army simply has nothing to offer them that they want badly enough to pledge loyalty.

Sebastian Junger fans may have an eerie feeling of déjà vu watching platoon soldiers building Camp Restrepo. They throw themselves directly into danger's path just like the swordfishermen in his breakthrough book, the mega-selling "*The Perfect Storm*," which was later adapted for the screen. Junger published *The Perfect Storm* in 1997, after several years as a war correspondent, starting in Bosnia in 1993, then Afghanistan in 1996, and in other notorious hotspots.

People in battle against epic enemies, whether natural or human, have always been at the heart of this multimedia journalist. "I primarily consider myself... Not an officer, certainly not a policy maker, but just a journalist. That's the part of my career that I'm most proud of."

By 2005, having spent more than a decade on the front lines of numerous battles as a print reporter, Junger was increasingly alarmed at the direction of the American fighting in Afghanistan. He'd initially supported the conflict but was growing disenchanted. He was fascinated by what the front line soldiers must have been experiencing in a mission so unclear and a climate so volatile; so he decided to pursue something he'd done little of in his war correspondence. He decided to try to get military approval to "embed" himself with a unit in Afghanistan, a vantage point that provides 24/7, unfettered and up close access to soldiers in the field. To do that, he needed an accredited sponsor, and since he had worked before for Vanity Fair magazine, he asked them to sponsor a series of print articles about troops in Afghanistan. He asked them to pick up costs for multiple reporting trips over the course of a year to the Afghan battlefield. And to his delight, Vanity Fair agreed.

"I thought, if I'm going to be out there on assignment with Vanity Fair that much, I might as well bring a video camera. I had shot a little video before in other conflicts. In combat, it's really hard to take notes, and you feel silly when you're doing it, and you can't read them afterwards anyway. So I just thought, combat's perfect for video cameras even if you don't know what you're doing, which I didn't," he recalls.

As a camera novice, he read the manuals like anybody else to try to get up to speed. But, to prevent shooting glitches due to his lack of experience, he decided to do it as low tech as possible—no tripod, no lights, and never, ever use manual settings—all "auto" only.

So he set out for Camp Restrepo, pen in one hand and camera in the other, as it were. "I had no idea what I was doing," he recalls. "I had this idea of doing a film and writing a book (at the same time). I know how to write a book but I don't know how to make a film, so I thought, I'm just going to start shooting video and I'll see what happens…"

But after that initial trip, he was in over his head. The verdict on the early material he gathered for this ambitious solo experiment was mixed. So, Junger reached out to other war correspondents for help. One of them was the affable, handsome and coolly focused British-American combat photographer Tim Hetherington. Hetherington, in his late 30s, had spent over a decade shooting some of west Africa's most brutal conflicts, and was known for his fearlessness, technical skills, and zeal for capturing potent wartime drama in his compositions.

Junger asked him to come and join him in the Korengal to see what he thought. "Tim understood the importance of the story, and what a good project it was, so he signed on immediately."

His new partner had also never made a film but had impressive visual chops, and had shot some video over the years. "He was just a very smart guy. Between the two of us, we really kind of had everything we needed. So all of a sudden, it went from a pipe dream on my part to a realistic possibility when he started."

The partnership grew stronger as the film evolved and proved invaluable for both. For most of the next year, Junger and Hetherington would alternate trips, working sometimes solo and sometimes together at the Camp.

Before *Restrepo*, Junger had shot "maybe, half an hour of video in my life." But through Hetherington, he picked up a few key pointers in the field. "I found out, for example, what a cutaway was. I didn't even know that .... You can tell when Tim told me what a cutaway was, because suddenly there's cutaways all over the place in the film. You can see me learning, but Tim did manual everything. If you see the camera's pulling focus on an extreme close-up, that's Tim's shot ... "

Junger applied the same approach to filmmaking that he'd used to turn himself into a best-selling author. Rely on instinct, and cherish the lessons he mined from his worst mistakes. "I never studied English or anything. I just ask myself, 'Why is that a great paragraph?' 'Why do I like it?' I did the same thing looking at my own video ... With shooting, I learned how to shoot for my editor ... I learned how to navigate how to frame a shot, when to zoom in and where to point the camera—that's all intuitive, not technical."

Hetherington used a basic Sony Z1 camera and Junger a Sony V1, and that's it. They even took the technically risky step of avoiding all external mics, opting for just the camera mic. "If it was hard to hear, we just got closer to the person who was speaking." The other "equipment" they left at home? Any kind of game plan going in. "We didn't have any kind of outline for the film.

Zero. We were just documenting as much as we could . . . . The last thing I want to do is to impose my assumptions and my ideas and my hopes about reality, onto reality."

Junger also had a philosophical objection to taking steps like pinning a lavaliere mic onto a soldier: believing that this makes him a performer, rather than just a soldier. "I think (going low-tech) made it feel more like war. I think if we had somehow figured out how to make it look and sound gorgeous, I think it would have been stunningly unreal, like a Hollywood movie."

They just had to hope that audiences would forgive any technical shortcomings and focus on the story instead. "It wasn't an artistic statement," Junger concedes. "We had to make this film with equipment we could carry on our backs, in combat, at 5–10,000 feet up in the mountains, while carrying everything else soldiers need . . . . we didn't even have a backup camera."

And, Hollywood movies, he notes with pride, are simply not in Junger's DNA. Even though Warner Brothers had sicked all its big budget guns to adapt Junger's "The Perfect Storm" for the screen (George Clooney, lavish storm scenes, etc.), Junger kept an arm's distance from the production. "They were actors, and when I was in the Korengal, it was reality. I don't even think about them (*Restrepo* and *The Perfect Storm*) in the same sentence."

Junger was determined to keep anything that felt Hollywood as far away as he could. "I knew the audience would be pretty forgiving for combat." When asked if bringing a camera in the room effectively turns everyone into an actor, his retort is instant: "Not in combat." As a rule, any scene where any of the soldiers seemed to be even remotely camera-aware, Junger left on the cutting room floor.

There is one particularly grueling and difficult-to-watch scene in the film where some viewers might take issue with Junger's claimed bias against performance. It is a scene where the soldiers seem to spontaneously writhe and dance, silly and gleefully, to a cheesy pop song. Given their setting and the film's serious tone and subject matter, it's jarring, and can feel like it's being played straight to the cameras.

Not at all, says Junger. "Combat is just a tenth of a percent of your experience in war. Most of the time the real enemy is boredom.... That scene is really understandable. They dance for the same reason teenage boys dance anywhere in the world to music. They're feeling young and good and powerful.... that's why I put it in the film."

The dancing scene is just one of many that lingers, unsettlingly, in the imagination, after the film is over. The film frequently keeps viewers on edge with a confident romp through scenes that swing from quiet and thoughtful, to tedious and futile, to hair-trigger violent. Low-fi production techniques are soon forgotten in the parade of tone changes. But Junger and Hetherington realized in looking at their footage that their audio could use an upgrade. They sensed that viewers might want some sonic calm amid the visual chaos, so they decided to supplement their in-field audio with highly produced studio interviews with key subjects, far from the battlefield.

After their deployment, the soldiers in the unit the filmmakers follow had a temporary layover in Italy. Junger initially wanted to use the same cameras they'd used in the field to record interviews with the men there in Italy, in a quiet room. But Hetherington would have none of it. He reasoned that the rough field audio needed to be augmented by state-of-the-art sound or viewers would struggle too much with it. So, unlike the ultra scrappy sound capture in Korengal, "we went overboard in the other direction," says Junger. At the base in Italy, they hired a DP, professional soundman, two high end cameras, lights and a studio. "It cost $50,000 of our own money, but we really did it to the max."

For viewers, the investment pays off. The studio interviews are crisp and clear, and the haunting black backdrops are mesmerizing. Now out of the deadly Valley, with its ruthless cycles of acute boredom and hair-trigger fears, the men are candid, reflective, emotional, and organized in their thoughts in ways we don't typically experience with them in battle mode.

The highly polished studio material is a vital counterpoint to the raw and spontaneous material the team captured in the field. Despite the frequent presence of their one or sometimes two cameras, there is an uncanny lack of self-awareness among the soldiers as they are trying to keep it all together in their highly endangered lives at Camp Restrepo. For Junger, there was the added challenge that he had to somehow capture this world for both print and visual audiences at the same time, juggling both pen and camera. Both the documentary and Vanity Fair craved a steady diet of images and insights on the lives of the *Restrepo* soldiers, and Junger had to frequently choose which tool was best for conveying which kinds of scenes.

"There were some situations that were perfect for note taking, like a conversation in the dark where guys are talking about their families or something. I mean, you don't want to turn the camera on then, right?" On the other hand, combat lent itself better to the lens. "There were really fast-paced conversations in daylight where you couldn't possibly keep up with your notebook. These are not emotionally laden situations so the camera doesn't feel intrusive. These scenes are perfect for a camera." Junger discovered that, in general, subtle and emotional want a pen and pad, while scenes and action prefer the lens.

"You can't film thoughts," he says. "I can write about the thoughts that I'm having, or the thoughts that someone else is having. But if you turn the camera on and ask a soldier, 'what are you feeling right now,' and that soldier's not articulate, it's not going to work on camera." Adding to the challenge is the reflexive macho that often accompanies the military mentality. "You ask a soldier if he's afraid, and he says no sir, I'm fine, even though he's lying. What do you do with that?"

In the end, Junger came to love the dual-media approach he brought to Camp Restrepo, feeling that despite some logistical challenges each medium enhanced the other. "The reason that I like print and film both is that I'm doing work that really affects different parts of the human brain. In one, I'm creating the illusion that you're actually there experiencing this thing. And in the other, in (print), I'm allowing you to really understand in a very deep, cognitive level what it's about."

And illusion, he found, was an important toe hold in the fast-changing and unpredictable realities he was experiencing at Camp Restrepo. The illusion he clung to passionately was one provided by the camera—it gave him a sense of safety, however misguided. The need to use the camera to capture the deadly action around him was a vital and maybe life-saving distraction, allowing him to focus on the filming tasks and shield himself from the deadly realities of the firefight. "It's not safety. I'm terrified. But I'm focused on something else: 'I better not screw it up—they're counting on me for the truth.' It's an act of denial."

And even though he was formally embedded with the troops, and was in the thick of the action, he was more vulnerable than all the rest—the only unarmed man on the battlefield. He accepted this blunt reality with typical stoicism: "Combat is an extremely practiced, coordinated thing. It's extremely formulaic. And if you don't know the formula, the plays, then another guy with a gun doesn't really help."

But outside of the occasional, bracing firefights and the doomed visits to nearby villages, much of daily life for the troops at Camp Restrepo is mundane. To give some extra visual punch to some of the scenes at Camp, many filmmakers might have opted to put themselves on screen—asking rhetorical questions, guiding viewers down certain narrative paths, and serving as a visual sounding board for the unfolding, multiple dramas. After all, Junger is handsome, emotive, and very well spoken. A commercially minded Executive Producer would very likely have at least been tempted to put Junger on the other side of the camera. This approach may be tempting to some but anathema to Junger. "I'm a journalist, and I'm just appalled at the recent trend, even in major networks like NBC, of turning the correspondent into the action hero."

Junger says the thought never crossed his mind. "The point of documentaries is to portray the world, and the documentarian is not the world. Unless you're specifically doing a film about yourself, that's fine. Otherwise, it's just self-preferential."

His rule-bound approach and sense of integrity are reflected in the film's sturdy structural feel, a highly organized look at a world that, in many ways, seems to possess scant form or logic. He believed so strongly in the material that he went into huge debt to make it. All the major broadcasters snubbed him when he tried to get the film funded before he left for Afghanistan. A&E, HBO, National Geographic? Pass, pass, pass.

"The hard part started when the deployment ended, which was when we had to come up with about $300,000 cash to make the film. Tim and I collectively took a deep breath, and put every spare dollar we had on the table, and paid for a one-year edit."

Then, film completed, all they needed was to find a buyer. National Geographic expressed renewed interest, but on condition of getting final cut. To Junger and Hetherington, this was a deal breaker. "We told (National Geographic) we'd walk away from the deal. That was really scary for us. This was right after the recession started, in 2009. We were making a feature length film about a war that everyone is sick of, and we're $300,000 in debt, and we're looking at another three hundred thousand, and we're ready to walk away from a deal that almost would've bailed us out of our financial hole. Out of editorial principle," Junger recalls. "But, they blinked first."

They ended up inking a TV deal with National Geographic, and when it came time to sell theatrical rights, the power balance would soon shift in their direction: they got into Sundance. Then, they won the Grand Jury Prize, and they were suddenly on more solid footing. National Geographic came in again, after the team's pitch: "Listen, we're going to find someone to partner with for theatrical. You should really do this, or it's going to be pretty weird." Perhaps a little boxed in, National Geographic bought the theatrical rights and agreed to keep the film's title (the broadcaster had hoped to rename it "Outpost Afghanistan."). Debts were paid, other festival awards were won, and, the icing on the cake, *Restrepo* was nominated for an Oscar for Documentary Feature for 2010.

Reflecting a few years later about the guts, or perhaps hubris, it took to walk away from National Geographic after they insisted on final cut, Junger realizes the dilemma hit him at his very core. "I risked my life for this movie. I risked my finances, and I almost lost my life doing it. And at that point you don't allow petty changes from a TV producer into your work," he says. "If I'm willing to risk my life for this, of course I'd risk my bank account."

The experience of making *Restrepo* would shake this veteran war journalist even more profoundly when his partner Tim died on April 20, 2011, less than a year after the film's theatrical release. "I just stopped being excited and started being sad after Tim got killed. I was married and it was kind of a co-decision with my wife. I didn't want to do that anymore. So, I'm done with war."

Something else he jettisoned along his journey covering soldiers and battle were the views of the US military that had shaped him since growing up in the anti-Vietnam War confines of Cambridge, Massachusetts in the 1970s. "I had a very liberal sort of stereotypical understanding of what the military is. The chain of command, the yes sir, no sir and all that. And actually the guys were incredibly smart, independently thinking guys. If you can't think on your feet, you'll have a bullet in your forehead."

Recovering from Hetherington's death, Junger threw himself into a film about his friend and partner. The well-received "Which Way is the Frontline From Here? The Life and Times of Tim Hetherington" (HBO, 2013) was Oscar-shortlisted.

Next, a quixotic trek that is also a tribute to Hetherington. In *The Last Patrol* (HBO), Junger takes on a journey he and Hetherington had planned. Accompanied by the journalist who was holding Tim's hand when he died, a photographer friend, and some of the soldiers featured in *Restrepo*, Junger and company made a 350-mile journey along the Amtrak lines across the US eastern seaboard, sleeping along the tracks and under bridges, in four seasons. "It was completely illegal. Sort of a high speed vagrancy," Junger recalls. "We had a 300+ mile conversation about how war is so hard to leave. How it's so hard to give up on war and return home."

10
Sergio

DIRECTOR AND PRODUCER
Greg Barker

Oscar short-listed, Best Documentary Feature (2010)

SUMMARY
Tells the story of the life and tragic death of the legendary and dashing United Nations diplomat, Sergio Vieira de Mello.

Greg Barker's riveting and gently hypnotic *Sergio* brings to vibrant life the rare gifts—courage, ego, and grit that characterized his film's outsized subject. Brazilian-born United Nations(UN) diplomat Sergio Vieira de Mello has been described as a mix of James Bond and Bobby Kennedy. And documentary producer and director Greg Barker proved more than ready to tackle the magisterial narrative that was the life of the late peacemaker, bon vivant, and global troubleshooting extraordinarian.

Intimate, candid interviews with those closest to Vieira de Mello weave around a gripping and potent dramatization of de Mello's final hours, trapped under mountains of rubble after a truck bomb detonated under his office. Barker's lean and impressionistic style brings us intimately into Vieira de Mello's anguished demise, with rescuers working desperately to try to save him.

After decades spent helping to calm warring sides in violent conflicts around the globe, Vieira de Mello was persuaded in 2003 to take on perhaps his biggest challenge of all—as the United Nations Secretary-General's Special Representative in Iraq. The Sisyphean task, in the early days of the US-led war in Iraq, instantly put him in the crosshairs of a bevy of well-armed enemies. One of those foes, interviewed by Barker at a secret location, would boast about the 2003 killing. When he died on August 19 that year, Vieira de Mello was just 55.

"He was one of those people that has a massive impact on everyone that they encounter," says Barker. "He was definitely a larger-than-life figure." His future seemed boundlessly bright, whether on the global stage or turning to a domestic life with the fiancé whose poignant insights provide much of the film's narrative engine.

Vieira de Mello was, in fact, in some ways just the kind of heroic and exotic figure Barker had been thinking about since his childhood in the bucolic suburbs of southern California. Barker's father, a Naval Officer, helped nurture those dreams. "My father was in the Pacific Fleet, and he would always send me back postcards from around the world. I just loved all the stories he'd tell about places and cities he'd go to and the people he'd meet. That's what got me interested in seeing the wider world."

Barker first considered stepping into his father's footsteps by joining the military. He got a Navy ROTC scholarship for college, but decided at the last minute that "I didn't want to work in a big bureaucracy." After graduating from George Washington University, he stayed on in the capitol and worked for a few years producing for C-SPAN and its stable of wonky talk shows. Solid experience, but he eventually found it limiting. So he set out for London, which felt like a kind of global capital. There, he got a Master's in International Relations and plunged into producing segments around the globe for CNN, BBC, and Reuters.

As a journalist, Barker took on some of recent history's most gritty conflicts. In the 1990s, he worked across the Middle East, in Eastern Europe, the former Yugoslavia and other hotspots. He toyed with the idea of becoming a full-time foreign correspondent in news, but grew disenchanted. "I could see a lot of the guys who did that, and how they were so energized during a crisis, and then I'd see them back in the CNN bureau in London later and they were covering the British rail system or something. They were bored out of their minds and just living for the next crisis." Not for me, he decided.

The news cycle's voracious appetite and short shelf life were not Barker's cup of tea, so he moved into creating long-format documentaries. He became a favored director for PBS's powerhouse "Frontline" series, bringing to the strand a disciplined and highly accessible storytelling flair that won him numerous awards. In the late 1990s, he began working on a Frontline special that would become his signature work to that point. His blunt and wrenching dissection of Rwanda's ruinous descent into genocide would yield the masterful *Ghosts of Rwanda* (2004). Many consider Barker's film to be *the* indelible chronicle of that 1994 tragedy.

Making the Rwanda film took 7 years, and while making it, he first heard about Sergio Vieira de Mello. Some UN staff he'd met in Rwanda went on to work for Vieira de Mello in East Timor and told Barker about his exploits and prowess. His deft navigation of the bloody conflict in tumultuous East Timor, which included his having to step in to directly administer the new nation's affairs, had spread his reputation for brilliant negotiating skills across the UN.

By the early 2000s, "he was on my radar," says Barker. Another key contact during his research on Rwanda was the then human rights activist and scholar, Samantha Power (who would in 2013 be named US Ambassador to the United Nations.) Power too had been fascinated by the legendary Brazilian and spoke about him with Barker. Right after he died in 2003, Power wrote a magazine article about Vieira de Mello that she would later turn into a book. Hearing about him on multiple fronts, Barker became fascinated by the man. "A lot of the people who I considered to be heroes for their work in Rwanda identified with Sergio, so I became interested in him too as an example of somebody who's immersed in the messy realities of the world, and how they can do that, get things done, and still retain their ideals."

Barker was entranced by Vieira de Mello's uncanny mix of expediency and imagination, a roll-up-your-sleeves style that stood down violent detractors and sought glimmers of humanity in even the most violent actors, always clawing for creative accord. "He was an amazing communicator, master manipulator, charismatic, smart, visionary," Barker says. "We need heroes in life."

So he acquired the rights to Samantha Power's book, "Sergio: One Man's Fight To Save The World," and the two decided to collaborate on a film. But pitching the story was eye-opening for Barker. "At that time, nobody wanted another film about Iraq. Everyone was 'Iraq'd out,' " he recalls. Barker had originally envisioned it as "the ultimate Iraq film, in a way. The bombing of the U.N. headquarters was really the beginning of the insurgency." But potential funders gave him a collective eye roll. Iraq fatigue had set in thick.

So Barker needed to re-tool his approach, to find a fresh way to spin the tale he wanted to tell. Instead of yet another Iraq documentary, he promised, it would just *happen* to be set in Iraq. And, not so much an anecdotal look at a single tragic bombing, the film would "tell the story about how we [Americans] take ourselves and our ideals into the world. It was about how we operate, about how we get ideas across after 9–11." And this approach did the trick. Wallets opened, checks were cut, and Barker was on his way.

Laying out the life of the diplomat would also allow Barker a way to wrestle with concepts that had long troubled him as an expatriate American. Especially during the George W. Bush administration, he was struck by how strongly so many non-Americans resisted the 43rd president's "us versus them mentality. His 'you're either for us or against us' attitude." To Barker, Vieira de Mello challenged that Manichean outlook in dramatic fashion. "For me what Sergio represented was a much more nuanced view of the world. A view that inhabited the shades of grey between right and wrong, between good and evil, and to try to make a difference within those shades of grey."

Barker was also adamant that, despite a story focused on a tragic killing, he wanted to create a hopeful and inspirational film. "I really clung on to that idea that it can't be some depressing downer film. We have to take some positive message out of it. Some redemption." Barker wanted to insure that his subject's brutal demise wouldn't overshadow his protean problem-solving skills.

And though *Sergio* does lay out multiple flattering vantage points on its subject's life and career, it's not all necessarily by design. Reflecting on the film a few years later, Barker is candid: "In retrospect I wanted more of his flaws. I wanted to speak more about the compromises he made along the way that were questionable." And in the course of his research, Barker encountered many people who told him—off camera—of such, laying out a much more mixed legacy. "There were a number of people in his life, particularly in his later years, who were very critical of Sergio and the way he conducted his business, and the way he conducted negotiations. Many in the human rights community did not like his tactics, though they wouldn't say so on camera because he was dead." In the end, reading between the lines, viewers can detect in the film "a little bit of his smarminess. He had a massive ego," says Barker.

Off camera, Barker heard frequent gripes about a peacemaker who shook hands with too many warmongers, an avowed romantic who womanizes relentlessly, and a bonhomie masking laser-sharp ambition. But even people who do appear in the film hold back when it comes to any criticism. The man trapped in the rubble with Vieira de Mello, Gil Loescher, had harbored longstanding ambivalence toward Vieira de Mello since the diplomat had helped broker a UN deal to forcibly return Vietnamese "boat people" back to their home country. "Gil was the fiercest critic over that. He thought it was awful." But once on camera, Loescher "pulled back. He just wouldn't go there." The duo's life and death drama in the rubble trumped their complicated history.

Barker was keenly aware of the conundrum he faced. Fans of *Sergio* would claim he uses the material he gets to his advantage, highlighting how deep heroism and negotiating brilliance require messy compromises and a savvy grasp of the gray areas that entangle foes in any conflict.

"He was a hustler. He would make deals. It's fascinating. In a dramatic version of his story, you would flush that out more. I mean, the guy's dead and all we have are the accounts of people who knew him. And if they won't go there, then it's hard to really capture that. The limits of documentary filmmaking, in a way … " Interviewing a bevy of experts on diplomacy might have turned up some more critical voices, but Barker eschewed those kinds of voices—not his style. Neither is a confrontational "gotcha" style favored by some documentary filmmakers, where subjects are manipulated to mouth what the filmmaker wants to hear. "I find that boring intellectually. I'd rather have the audience reach their own conclusions. I tend to ask questions that are more open-ended," he explains.

The classically confrontational "60 Minutes" approach also goes against something deeper in Barker. When a filmmaker confronts a wrongdoer with a "Why did you commit crime X?" question, the implication is that the filmmaker would have made a different choice. But Barker isn't certain. "I'm never sure how I would have behaved if I was in that person's shoes," he concedes. "I have nothing to prove to the audience that I'm more righteous than the interviewee … let's learn from mistakes people made rather than try to feel morally superior." Barker goes back to his research on the horrors in Rwanda to underscore his point. During the 1994 massacres, Barker recalls, America's "most open-minded, liberal and far-sighted foreign policy officials" looked away as more than 800,000 people were massacred in three months.

Did those policy makers simply not care? No, says Barker. "They were convinced (doing nothing) was doing the right thing."

For his interviews for *Sergio*, Barker wanted solely first person recollections from those who knew him best and at critical junctures of his life. And Barker was also keen to move away from the conventional journalistic "balance for its own sake" approach: i.e. if someone criticizes something, then next find a backer, etc. "If I'd been making this film for a 'Frontline,'" he acknowledges, "it would have been a totally different film."

To help piece together the moments that lead to his tragic end, Barker had the invaluable framework of Samantha's Powers' book to use as a starting point. By acquiring the documentary rights to the book, Barker also secured access to her voluminous world of contacts. She'd interviewed some 600 people for the book.

"The book can definitely help. It often helps getting a doc off the ground because it validates it in a way," he says. But Barker found, as he has with other films he's made that were drawn from books, that a book can be a great door-opener but not a guarantor of any special access.

"The reality is that people were not going to do the film because they talked to Samantha for the book. They were going to do it or not do it because they believed in my vision for it," explains Barker. In some cases—someone hates the book or how they're portrayed in it, for example—wielding a book can even be a drawback. Or, they may feel they've already told the author all they have to say on the subject and aren't up for another re-hash. "It can cut all different ways.... the film has to stand on its own in terms of content and access. It's really just the starting point."

In the end, Barker was extremely pleased with the collaboration. At the time they were making the film, Power was already a well-known author, a popular fixture on the college lecture circuit and a consultant for the then US Senator from Illinois, Barack Obama. "It's a give-and-take. The movie is different than the book but she loved it in the end. It would have never happened without her."

Together, they secured a powerhouse group of raconteurs, including a wide range of UN colleagues and policy titans who knew Vieira De Mello, including top US diplomat Richard Holbrooke, ex-British Premier Tony Blair and former US Secretary of State Condoleeza Rice. Barker felt the unusual central character demanded an imaginative way of story-telling and interviewing. So instead of the usual talking head set up, he experimented. At first, he tried a technique pioneered by veteran documentary visionary Errol Morris, which uses a set up similar to two Teleprompters and allows interviewer and subject to look at one another on a screen. "But I hated it," recalls Barker. "I could see them, but I had no sense of the texture. You couldn't feel the energy. We did one interview like that which we didn't use."

So Barker toyed further. He found he liked sitting directly below the camera and slightly far away from the subject. "It looks like they're looking at the camera and you still have that connection with them. It's a really uncomfortable way to sit, particularly for long interviews, but it worked. It gave me the look I wanted, and the physical presence I needed to connect with people." The interview space is dark, quiet, and relaxing for the subject (if not the interviewer!), and the outside world "melts away." Barker has used the technique for every film he's made since.

Barker got some good advice from one of his producers, Passion Pictures' John Battsek, early on as he wrestled with how to approach the material and the story arc. "John really encouraged me to start the edit with a handful of key interviews. He said, 'Once you get enough, just start cutting. And then you'll discover the film through that.'"

Barker hadn't taken this exact tack before but was eager to try. So he and his crew set out to interview right away Carolina Larriera, Vieira de Mello's fiancé and the rescuers who tried to take Vieira de Mello out of the rubble. With these in place, the story flowed from there. And though they'd relied initially on funding from a variety of foundations and investors to get started, during production HBO came on board for US rights. BBC then came on board for the UK rights, followed by additional funders to help finish it.

Once the structure of the film was in place, built around the interviews, Barker and his team would take on one of the film's biggest challenges of all—the dramatizations of Vieira de Mello's three-hour long struggle to survive, deep in the rubble of the collapsed building. He turned to a noted commercial still photographer (and his brother-in-law) Patrick Fraser to act as lead shooter for the two days of dramatizations. He struggled with casting for the two key people who would lead the rescue efforts of Gil Loescher and Vieira de Mello. The only way the rescuers, William von Zehle and Andre Valentine, could keep Gil Loescher alive had been to cut off both of his legs, right in the rubble. Vieira de Mello was just behind him and they hoped to hoist Loescher out to safety and then work on freeing Vieira de Mello. But by the time they were able to gain full access to Vieira de Mello, he had died from his internal injuries.

The crushed building the men lay under was so unstable and cramped and the experience—amputation, trying to rescue dying people under rubble—so idiosyncratic and alien that it was very difficult to find people who could pull that off with credibility. But then Barker had an idea. How about asking the rescuers themselves to re-create those incidents on camera? To Barker's surprise and delight, both agreed to do it.

Barker and Fraser tinkered with the low light and cramped quarters of the set for days before settling on a set up they liked. Fraser would shoot the main 16 mm camera, and Barker would shoot both a secondary 16 mm, and an 8 mm. Barker was very aware of the downsides of dramatizations—the risks of looking hokey or maudlin ran very high. They also needed to capture a paradoxical mood, involving frenzy and chaos among searchers just outside the rubble and a slow, suffocating deadness closing in on the men inside. Barker had access to some very powerful archival footage shot inside the building just after the blast, which he would need to integrate with the dramatizations he was shooting. "It was all very raw," he recalls, summing up the daunting challenges they faced on those shoot days. One of the most difficult to watch scenes in *Sergio* is a hysterical Carolina Larriera begging rescuers to let her get close enough to the rubble so that she can speak to her fiancé. Their heartbreaking expressions of love to each other—she seeming to speak into towers of ragged concrete and he doomed inside—linger long after the film is over.

The stakes and perils for Barker and his team shooting these scenes were high, as were emotions on the set. "It was an extremely emotional moment for all of us because Bill and Andre (the two rescuers) were very, very much in that moment, which was the most intense moment of their lives," recalls Barker. To accommodate the potent emotional weight on set, Barker and Fraser would stop frequently and allow the "actors" to physically and mentally re-group and summon up the presence to carry on.

And as the film winds down, characters reveal more details that highlight the magnitude of the tragedy. Larriera reveals she and he had bought their airline tickets to start their new life in Brazil just the night before the bombing. Another interviewee talks about how Vieira de Mello himself had always wanted the UN compound in Baghdad to appear to welcome the public and not to appear as a far-away fortress of occupation. So, security at the compound was lighter than others had urged and made it relatively easy for a determined truck bomber to drive right up to the compound. Samantha Power, assessing the tragedy, is brought close to tears as she relates how pathetically underprepared the UN mission was for dealing with a tragedy such as this. The rescuers were attempting a nearly impossible task, using for "equipment" little more than a woman's handbag found in the dirt and a piece of rope.

Barker makes clear that this epic figure died both painfully and needlessly.

In all, Barker would shoot for about 10 months and then edit for another eight. *Sergio* got into Sundance for 2009, to rapturous reviews. The US economy was cratering at the time, and Barker was relieved to have HBO already on board. At Sundance, he could enjoy himself—he wasn't looking to strike a deal. From a marketing standpoint, Barker knew that *Sergio* would be a tough sell since so few people knew the subject. "He's not, like, a Michael Jordan. It's more like, 'who is this guy? Why should I care?'" So, it was a huge help to get to rely on the marketing wizards at HBO to help the film break through.

Later that year, an Oscar short-listing nod was icing on the cake. Barker also got to screen *Sergio* for some powerhouse audiences, including an A-list event in Washington for 600 people who included Treasury Secretary Larry Summers, Supreme Court Justice Elena Kagan, and numerous State Department and White House officials. He also got to screen the film for Vieira de Mello's closest insiders and admirers at the UN General Assembly. An auditorium filled with countless ambassadors and diplomats, many of them his personal friends, choked up at the portrayal of the man whom many had pegged as a strong candidate for the Secretary-General's job some day.

HBO, for its part, offered Barker another high-profile film after *Sergio*, the superb *Manhunt*, about the search for Osama Bin Laden, which Barker finished in 2013.

Barker also later optioned the dramatic rights to Samantha Power's book about Vieira de Mello, after the rights lapsed with a previous holder. He's co-writing the script for the narrative film and would direct it. "I think it's a potentially Oscar-winning role for somebody. It's a phenomenal character."

11

Maya Lin: A Strong Clear Vision

DIRECTOR AND PRODUCER
Frieda Lee Mock

Oscar Winner, Best Documentary Feature (1994)

SUMMARY
*The fascinating life and career of young architect Maya Lin,
designer of the Vietnam Veteran Memorial, the Civil Rights Memorial
and other powerful public art projects.*

When a group of Vietnam War veterans in the early 1980s launched a nationwide, blind competition to design a memorial in Washington, D.C., there was no telling what kinds of submissions would come in. The War had ended only a few years earlier, in 1975. Memories on all sides of the battle were still acute and raw, and some 58,000 American soldiers lay in graves.

Artists, architects, and designers from across the country submitted an eclectic array of designs, some 1,400 in total, ranging from the grandiose and somber to the odd and even silly. It was thought to be the largest design contest in US history.

But there was one design that the Commission charged with picking the winner kept coming back to—a simple, black, v-shaped and low-slung wall that would have every fallen soldier's name etched into it. Many of the country's leading designers had submitted entries, and the judges had every reason to believe that one of these heavy weight entries would win. But committee members were stunned when they looked at the return address for entry number 1,026, the design they would pick. It was an address for student housing at Yale University.

When the winner of the contest was revealed, there was a collective gasp: a 21-year-old undergraduate architecture student named Maya Lin. Lin herself thought she had little to no chance of winning, believing that her design's simplicity and focus on the grim outcome of battle, rather than its heroic qualities, would doom it. Right when both winner and design were announced publicly, anger and heated rebuttals began flying in all directions.

Quickly, veterans groups, designers, architects, and politicians staked out positions on both design and designer, and the debate turned vitriolic. Critics sometimes hurled racially loaded diatribes against Lin, a second generation Chinese-American.

Perhaps it was inevitable that the battle lines of a War that had so intensely divided the American public would be re-drawn for a Memorial to remember it by.

Sitting in her mother's kitchen in San Francisco sipping coffee one morning in 1981, Frieda Lee Mock was riveted by a newspaper article about the controversy.

"Some veterans thought they'd get the typical heroic statue, and instead they got this thing... this new, breakthrough design made by this unknown, inexperienced person. I think when some first saw Lin, they thought she was Vietnamese, and that (the Commission) was giving it to her in deference to the War," recalls Mock, a Los Angeles-based documentary filmmaker.

Mock was struck by the young architect's ways of dealing with the controversies launched by her work. "Her voice and her attitude—they were incredible. Her voice just cut through a lot of the shrill nonsense being said about her design. It just cut through like a laser," says Mock.

Mock was struck by Lin's pithy and often humorous retorts to her (mostly male) critics and her "independent, pure spirit." When foes suggested she put a flagpole in the middle of the design, she shot back that it was a Memorial—not a golf course. Others told her to make it white, so it would look like the other statues on the Capitol Mall. No, she said. Black will work. Trust me. "It's like you're asking me to paint a mustache on the Mona Lisa," as Mock sums up Lin's responses to her critics.

Some critics objected to the way the fallen soldiers' names would be inscribed—by year of death, rather than all of them laid out alphabetically. Lin pointed out that the mass alphabetical format was prone to multiple listings of common names (i.e. "John Smith, John Smith ... ") Lin argued that her way of grouping names would make it less confusing for visitors unable to discern which John Smith, say, was *their* John Smith. In the hot seat, the college student proved again and again that she had both anticipated many of the critiques lobbed her way and was more than ready to defend her creative vision.

For filmmaker Mock, the brewing David and Goliath tale, with its stalwart central character, was riveting. "She looks about 14 years old. But she's a powerful person. She's very clear and strong in standing up for what she believes .... There was something so seminal and basic in that story. It really resonated at my core."

The story planted a seed in her creative mind. Mock had been making documentaries for some of the handful of documentary production companies that thrived at the time, notably the legendary David L. Wolper Productions. But she had also been wanting to set out and make a film on her own, when the story and timing were right.

Fast forward to 1989, and Maya Lin would again turn on a light bulb for Mock. The Vietnam Memorial had been dedicated in 1982 to widespread acclaim, and Lin was now developing another grand Memorial, this one about Civil Rights, to be built in the Deep South. "I just went 'bingo!'. The idea came to me that that might be interesting to do a film about these big ideas—War and Race—and to see how she expresses them not in a monograph or an essay, but in 3-dimensional form." Invigorating Mock even more, Lin said the Civil Rights Memorial would be her last memorial. Time was running out. The table was set.

"Right away I wrote her a letter saying I've done these kinds of films, and I'm interested in doing a film about your creative process and your work. And I thought I'd never hear from her. And a few days later I get this call from New York, and she says, 'Ok, let's do it.' I couldn't believe it. And I just thought to myself, ok, now what?"

So she and her partner, fellow filmmaker Terry Sanders, next formed a non-profit company, the American Film Foundation, to receive grants for films. Then she hit the grant-writing trail, asking for funds from any place she could think of—the National Endowment for the Arts, the National Endowment for the Humanities, the Corporation For Public Broadcasting, the Paul Robeson Fund, and others. It's time-consuming and nerve-wracking work, but Mock tried to block all the stress out and plow ahead. "I was dogged, like Sisyphus. You just believe it's going to get done, and you just say, 'I will raise the money.'"

But application and funding cycles for funds like these are notoriously drawn out, and outcomes are hard to predict. Mock realized she'd need to take on for-hire work as needed while making the *Maya Lin* film to make ends meet. So she and Sanders also created a for-profit entity (Sanders and Mock Productions) to house for-profit work. Even when the film began to rake in funds on the grant circuit, she still had to take whatever for-hire work she could get throughout the production.

Fund-raising would be a chore she'd have to work at for the entire production. There would not likely ever be a point where she could say, "I have enough money. I'm set." In one especially poignant episode, she recalls driving down to visit a potential donor. "I heard that a Chinese-American woman in

Laguna Beach was supportive of art projects and interested in the Maya film. So I walk into this big fancy place by the ocean and she says, 'You know what. My husband has to have major surgery on his teeth. I can't put money into the film.' I was like, oh no, your husband doesn't need that operation!" she recalls ruefully. "And I tried convincing her that the Maya film was more important than oral surgery! That's just life as an independent filmmaker. You just have to laugh at yourself later on."

Breaking away from the comfort of the production company, with its cozy infrastructure and regular paychecks, was unnerving. "Sometimes I thought, 'why did I do that?' ... It's a leap of faith, and I just went with this crazy idea. I wanted to do a film about this artist, and bookend it with war and race, and then that would be it." Mock was also getting weary of the strict durations and formatting rules for television documentaries and craved more creative freedom.

She hoped for a quick production schedule and then planned to move on to other projects. But what she hadn't counted on was the protean imagination of her subject. In their early meetings, Lin shared with Mock a whole raft of projects, going way beyond just the Civil Rights Memorial. "She was doing a project on peace, one on women, one on ecology ... And I thought, wow, she's covering all the big 'isms' of our time! I said, well, this looks like it's going to be a bigger film."

She quickly realized that to do her subject justice on screen, a quick turn-around production was simply not in the cards. Grand, controversial memorials, like any home construction project, can take years to make and delays are common. But Mock also knew she needed a goal line, a thematic way to wrap up her film. So Mock made the decision to include the big "ism" projects on Lin's drawing board at the time she started to film and then aim to finish her film at the same time as Lin was wrapping up those works.

But filming an artist creating massive, labor-intensive work doesn't lend itself to tidy production schedules. Some of Lin's work involved physically designing works and walking around projects in progress. These lent themselves well to filming. Other aspects, such as meetings and the like, were less camera friendly.

But Mock made the decision early on that she would shoot with Lin when her subject was open to it and to defer to Lin when the designer said no. Mock would never try to change her subject's mind in order to get material she wanted—it would be improvised. "As an artist, she was driven by what she felt she needed to do, so you, as a filmmaker coming into her life, needed to adjust to her schedule and her needs." This made for a buoyant rapport between Mock and Lin but presented challenges as well.

"I accepted that we were basically 'on call' to her," Mock explains about the approach she brought to the *Maya Lin* film and every one she's done since. "Maya's in New York, and I'm on the West Coast, ready to jump on the plane. To me, the feeling is, we're not paying you for your time." Literally and figuratively, says Mock, "(We filmmakers) are really guests in your home."

In one instance, Mock wanted to capture a scene of Lin with her mother, wanting to personalize her portrait and show viewers more of her life off the construction site and drafting table. Lin's response: "I don't think you'd be showing (celebrated architect) Frank Gehry with his mother, would you?" Lin passed. And rather than pressing, as some filmmakers might have done, Mock let it go. "I was very conscious about that aspect, about making a film about a person who's made a major contribution and who happens to be female, and who happens to be Asian, but without focusing on that," Mock explains. Mock says she's conscious of what she considers a double standard in how male and female characters are portrayed in film and wanted to underscore the focus on Lin's work.

On a couple of occasions, Lin agreed to a shoot but then backed out. Mock took it in stride, but at times her crew was puzzled. "Doesn't she know you're paying people, and now she's sayings no, we can't film today?" her crew sometimes asked Mock. To Mock, it's a question of balancing respect for her subject with her own creative agenda. "You're always kind of negotiating. You have to be sensitive, but know you're intruding."

It's about keeping the relationship with her subject strong but also being deferential to them to underscore the distance needed between her and her subject. "You're not best friends," she says, but after all, "you are intimate in their lives because you're hanging around a lot. And they have to trust you that you're not going to embarrass them." Maintaining distance with her subject fit into one of Mock's broader goals: keep the film focused on her work, not her personal life. "You can see there were issues of race, sexism, and ageism—she was so young. The challenge was to balance those issues within the larger story of her creative process and work."

Guidelines for her relationship with Lin in place, Mock had to come up with a structure to organize the film. She began gathering archival footage of the Vietnam Veterans Memorial material that caught her attention in the first place—the bidding contest, the controversies, and ultimately its dedication in 1982. She would start the film with that material. "The most powerful story for Maya is absolutely the Vietnam Memorial. That war affected millions of people's lives, and she's an important figure in that story. The Vietnam Memorial is what people understand and what people are emotionally connected to," says Mock of her thinking on the film's structure.

To wrap up the film, she'd film vérité material focused on Lin's design for the Civil Rights Memorial. Since that work was ongoing, and there was far less controversy attached to it, she figured that this second memorial would be a strong vantage point for exploring Lin's creative process via vérité shooting.

But the Civil Rights Memorial was nearly complete when she began to shoot, and the dedication would take place in early November 1989; so she had to rush to gather funds to shoot the dedication and some of the work on it that took place just before.

The other big deadline looming, and one which she hoped could generate some interesting material, was the 10th anniversary of the Vietnam Memorial coming up in 1992. The Memorial's dedication in 1982 had been highly fraught. It featured a tense and tentative series of speeches, the relegation of Lin to near anonymity in the crowd, and the very visible snubbing of the event by President Ronald Reagan.

But by 1992, the controversy had ebbed, with some of the former foes in 1982 having made peace. Lin was given a very gracious and emotional introduction, and it was as if an armistice was being signed right on the spot. "You keep this Wall alive," she told the assembled, bringing a rousing, long overdue, ovation.

For Mock, the 1992 anniversary was a perfect bookend. She opens the film with emotional and moving scenes of veterans seeing the Memorial for the first time, at its dedication in 1982. Many are overcome and in tears, reliving painful memories and seemingly overwhelmed with gratitude that a country that had for so long shunned them was now honoring them so grandly. By 1992, at film's end, Lin is beaming at the dais, seemingly taken over by emotion herself, and it is as if all parties had emerged from shadows. For Mock, the elegant top and bottom become like an envelope into which she slips the riveting journey that took her subject from lightning rod to visionary.

Mock finished her film in late 1994 and submitted it to the new-ish Sundance film festival (started in 1985). Thumbs down. Undeterred, she submitted it for Oscar consideration, and to her astonishment, the film was nominated for Best Documentary Feature. She hadn't submitted the film at that point to any other festivals, but had set up, on her own, a handful of mostly art house screenings and a few events. When she won the Oscar, theaters called to ask for more screenings and festivals wanted it too. And so her company started Ocean Releasing and launched a nationwide theatrical and festival run. "Looking back, I think I was pretty naïve about it all. But the

Oscar really helped, of course, in terms of the marketing and everything. It was great," Mock says.

Then, having shown she could pull off a successful and emotional film, centered on a challenging story and subject matter, funders began to call her. "The Oscar definitely opened doors, and made people think, oh, we can trust this filmmaker with this kind of material." One such group who approached her were graduates of the Air Force Academy. They asked her to make a film about Vietnam War combat pilot POWs and said they would fund the entire film.

That film would become *Return with Honor*, (1999), co-directed with Terry Sanders and would get a big boost when fellow Oscar winner Tom Hanks and his company offered to present the film theatrically and to narrate an introduction for its TV broadcast. Since then, the duo has received other Oscar nominations and has gone on to create successful films on myriad stories and subjects.

"Looking back on it all, the way we made 'Maya' was crazy. Afterwards I said, 'I'm not going to do that again, an independent film taking 5 years.' But then, of course, I did it again. And again, and again."

12

Sound and Fury

DIRECTOR AND PRODUCER

Josh Aronson

PRODUCER

Roger Weisberg

Oscar Nomination, Best Documentary Feature—2000

SUMMARY

*An exploration of the world of deafness via a family torn apart
by their dramatically different approaches to their deaf children.
Is deafness a disability, or a chosen culture and lifestyle?*

"This is a story that just came to me instantly," recalls Josh Aronson. "It was just one of those lucky things." Aronson's sudden burst of inspiration came to him one afternoon in the mid-1990s walking down the street in Santa Monica, California. The light bulb went off in the most unlikely way and would end up re-shaping his world views and career, snagging an Oscar nomination just a few years later.

Aronson had been making a fine living creating music videos, televisior pilots and commercials, but was growing weary of the obsessiven and high pressure atmosphere. He was keen to take on his first fe documentary, and he was actively looking for a subject that woul his interest and sustain it over the years he knew it would take recently had a brief experience in the world of the deaf, one that stayed with him. He'd shot a live one-woman show that included, as many such shows do, a woman signing on the side of the stage. "It was my first real contact with signing and I thought it was just beautiful," he says. "Deaf people are so comfortable in that universe."

He was walking that day with a friend who'd worked with a company that made cochlear implants, surgically implanted devices that can dramatically improve hearing for the deaf. Deafness, as it happened, was on the minds of both of them that day, and when one of them mentioned "cochlear implants," suddenly a woman walking in front of them turned around and exclaimed: "I have a cochlear implant!"

"She told us the cochlear implant changed her life because it had allowed her, for the first time in 30 years, to talk on the telephone and do various other things," recalls Aronson. The woman rattled off other benefits to her newly recovered hearing but then ended that thought with a coda that stopped Aronson in his tracks. The big drawback to the implant, she confessed, was that she lost all of her friends.

"What?" asked an incredulous Aronson. How so? "She told us that all of her deaf, signing-culture friends now shunned her. And she told me a three-minute version of the deaf community's hostility toward the cochlear implant. I saw my film in a flash," he says. "She had described a culture of people that are opposed to this technology that could effectively allow a deaf child to function in a hearing world."

Aronson had never seriously considered any such downsides to the cochlear implant. Just as with most hearing people, deafness is something 'e'd generally considered a "disability," and a device to address it, he assumed, ild be welcomed. He was shocked to realize how off base this assumption Je knew right then that he wanted to make a film about this fascinating nvulsing the deaf world. "This is a conflict of the first order. I just saw 'n a flash. It took 5 years to make, but I saw it in a flash."

But instead of reaching for a camera, Aronson hit the books, burying himself in articles and literature about deafness for the next six months. He'd be taking on a first feature documentary and on a topic he knew next to nothing about. So he barricaded himself away to try to get up to speed on the history of deaf culture and of the hearing world's often misguided or even cruel attempts to "fix" deafness. "I was fascinated by this subject. It just gripped me by the throat," recalls Aronson. How, he wanted to know, could this community that he'd long viewed through rosy lenses, have turned against itself so dramatically?

He also wanted to reach out and talk to people on all sides of the deaf world and those involved in the cochlear implant debate. But as an outsider from the hearing world, he found himself hitting brick walls, with people not wanting to be fully candid and open with him. "Both sides were resistant to me," Aronson explains. "The deaf culture/signing world assumed I was some hearing guy who would implant my child in a heart beat and they didn't want anything to do with me … Others thought I would fall in love with cute little deaf and signing children, and the beauty of sign, and I wouldn't take cochlear implants seriously."

Boxed in, he realized he needed a reliable guide who could help him gain entry to and navigate both worlds. Through connections, he came upon New York University film graduate Jackie Roth, who was almost deaf, and the child of deaf parents who spoke well and signed fluently. "I invited her to be my guide, my muse, because she knew everyone on all sides of the fence, and she was accepted on all sides. So she signed on as my Associate Producer (later becoming Coordinating Producer). And becau of her, now I had access."

After months of research, persistent questioning and pressing the the wide-ranging deaf world, he felt like he had a solid handle on raging debate. Now all he lacked was money to make the commercial directing years, he'd been able to sock away som in the much lower-budget documentary world, he quickly realized the money wasn't nearly going to be enough.

Enter Roger Weisberg. "I was in the middle of producing a PBS film when I got a call out of the blue from Josh Aronson," recalls the veteran PBS producer and prodigious fundraiser. Aronson wanted Weisberg's producing skills, and fundraising chops. "I didn't think I could become involved, but the material was so intriguing. When he showed me one of the prospective subjects, who wept when she had a hearing child because she wanted this child to belong to the deaf world, to be able to sign and communicate with her parents.... I had never really encountered that expression of identity, and it was that experience, and meeting and liking Josh, that ultimately won me over."

Weisberg signed on as Producer and set out to raise funds. Aronson was now freed up to concentrate on getting his first feature documentary off the ground without simultaneously having to pass around the hat for money. Weisberg had a vast track record in fundraising, licensing, and distribution for PBS material—a perfect complement to a director with creative chops but little documentary experience. But as Weisberg was representing the film to PBS, he needed some control as well as his director, and so the two partners agreed that in the final edit of the film, they had to come to consensus before the final film went out.

Weisberg and Aronson viewed the fundamentals of the film in the same way, intent on squelching any biases they may have brought to the film and to make sure that fairness to all sides would prevail. Weisberg admits that, at least initially, he "couldn't understand why a parent wouldn't want a child to have the benefits of being able to be part of the deaf culture, but be able to function in the hearing world, to be able to communicate." But viewers feel in and fury their deep commitment to balance and an open mind attuned e bitterest adversaries. Regardless of any opinions they brought to the they'd face "we were just determined to present every character's 'ly as we could," says Weisberg.

Just weeks after the duo joined forces, they began casting in earnest and shooting. "We often make stupid business decisions because we're passionate about the subjects we address. With this one, we sort of threw ourselves into it and decided to just play catch up with the funding," says Weisberg. It was a calculated roll-of-the-dice, born of confidence about the material—or perhaps hubris. "I was a little bit cocky because I had always been able to cover the cost of my production with fundraising, and I just felt I could do it again," Weisberg explains.

Aronson's original plan had always been to find an array of characters spanning the identity spectrum of the deaf world—from committed pro-cochlear implant "oralists" who thought sign language was a dead end for deaf people, to deaf culture signers who felt the implant was tantamount to genocide in the deaf world.

Aronson and Weisberg knew that they'd need an extraordinary cast of characters to justify their confidence and to deliver the kind of emotionally powerful drama they knew was there to tap. So Associate Producer Julie Sacks helped them expand the search Aronson had been on for months, pounding the pavement at deaf organizations and schools, audiologists, and implant surgeons.

The dream was to find a couple who had a child who was deaf and to follow them for a year as they explored all the different options available to raising their deaf child. The plan was that their journey would weave through the stories of several other characters who'd been deaf since childhood and had made different choices about how to live with their deafness. The hope was that this family would live near New York to facilitate frequent and spur-of-the-moment shooting near where they lived.

Then one day during the search, Julie Sacks called Aronson and said had turned up a really special and unusual family. Even though they d the profile she had been asked to search for, Sacks pressed him to m So, Aronson headed out to Long Island to meet the Artinian fa minutes, he felt he'd struck gold. "I looked at this entire extended family sitting around the grandparents' living room and realized that right in front of me was the entire story I had seen from the outset on that street in Santa Monica. Their story was a microcosm of the battle going on in the deaf world in one family. It was a no-brainer, if I could get their permission and earn their trust."

The family featured two married brothers, one deaf and one hearing but each with deaf children. Chris, the hearing brother, had twins, one hearing and one—Peter—deaf. Chris and his wife had made the decision to implant their son. Peter, the deaf brother, and his deaf wife passionately celebrated their family's place in the deaf world. And when they heard that Chris was implanting his child, they were incensed. But in the course of the film, their 5-year-old daughter, Heather, announced she too wanted an implant. Peter and Nita dutifully looked into the possibility, ultimately choosing against the implant for their child.

"We were handed on a silver platter this narrative that had conflict, great characters," Weisberg exults, still relishing the discovery. "We couldn't have asked for anything more. Their story really encapsulated the broader battle that was being waged in the deaf community." Jackpot. The Artinians disagreed with each other's choices, passionately and volubly. Aronson knew from the get-go he wanted the film to be vérité-driven, giving viewers a raw, spontaneous, and under-the-hood look inside truly fascinating moral fault lines.

Aronson connected closely to the family and was embraced by them. Spending lots of time with the families, both planned and unplanned, helped break down any barriers they might have had. He ultimately felt like a part of ▸e family and felt accepted by them. "I feel as if they trusted that l was there to ◦ each side to give their perspective and defense of their choices for their ◦n. These were highly emotional people making decisions that would ◦ir children's identity for a lifetime. So it was raw and wonderfully

The characters even ended up giving Aronson a heads-up when there were situations coming up where there were likely to be important discussions or camera-worthy sparks flying between family members. For example, one character called Aronson before a 4th of July picnic to say "I'm going to risk everything and give [other family members] a piece of my mind at the picnic. Do you want me to wait till you are there to shoot?" Says Weisberg, "It was a very close collaboration. We knew when we needed to show up."

To maintain comity, they also used as small a crew as they could and tried whenever possible to use the same crews. And even though fly-on-the-wall vérité was their modus operandi, they "couldn't resist stoking the flames from time to time to get the discussions going," says Weisberg. At points when the different camps in the family weren't speaking, the filmmakers sometimes helped steer them to get together. "Because they were making this film with us as our colleagues, they agreed," explains Aronson.

Intimate access like this breeds candor, but it also risks manipulation. Each family had a very clear agenda, and the filmmakers were well aware of the characters' goals. The characters' agendas motivated the actions and words that give the film shape and buoyancy, but the filmmakers took pains not to let themselves get taken advantage of. "I don't think we were manipulated," says Weisberg. "For example, I think it's possible that the grandmother felt that we were on her side, but I think the son she was arguing against probably thought that we were on his side too."

Aronson was acutely aware of the responsibility they took on by getting such unfettered access to this high stakes family feud. If family members had accused him of taking sides, it would have jeopardized not just the film but also the psychological well-being of an extended family about whom the filmmakers cared enormously. Responsibility was both a burden and a safeguard.

The moral weight the filmmakers carried kept them on their toes, as did the technical challenges of sound capture in the deaf world. Capturing their conversations required watching them; so, depending on the nature and scale of the scene, they would use one or more interpreters giving simultaneous translations to the filmmakers. Ideally, they wanted the translation to also be going to the cinematographer so he or she could follow the action better. But that often caused headaches for the shooters, who found it enormously distracting, and they had to just "wing it" as best they could.

Translation was enormously tricky and sometimes involved as many as a dozen people signing at or almost at the same time. Even simple interviews were fraught. Aronson used two mics—one for the simultaneous interpretation of the signer, as Aronson's signing was good but not usually quite up to the task; and another mic to capture the muffled but very physical and critical sounds that even signers make and which are key to communication—gesticulations, murmurs, fingers striking the body, and the like.

And then after all the translations are captured, they still needed to be precisely and professionally translated afterwards since live translation is—in any language—rarely exact. A mis-translated word or phrase could also cause enormous bad feelings, so attention to the work—time-consuming and expensive—was paramount. "Sometimes it wasn't until after the fact that we knew what we really had because we weren't able to get that simultaneous translation a hundred percent of the time," says Weisberg. And professionally translated material would often force them to re-cut scenes, to insure that everything was in sync. "It was incredibly complicated. It gave me such a headache," Aronson sighs, recalling the time with a weary smile.

But Aronson had enormous support from all sides, vital for a feature documentary rookie like himself. When money was tight, Weisberg told him not to sweat it. "'If you think you need a scene, go do it. Don't worry about it. I'll get the money,' Roger would say to me. He was so supportive. It was wonderful," says Aronson. With a Producer happy to help find funding for many of his creative desires, "It was a dream team for my first time out," beams Aronson.

The rookie struck big with *Sound and Fury*, but there is one regret that still gnaws at him. He wishes the film looked better. "Sometimes it looks like a home movie," he says now, a bit chagrined considering he came from the ultra-slick visual medium of commercials. Some of the film does have a mushy, soft focus look, and interviews are sometimes done with unimaginative backdrops. Aronson attributes the film's occasionally amateurish visual feel to his inability "to sacrifice the scene to shoot in better light, or to find a better place to shoot. We were in houses that had nowhere nice to shoot in, and we just went with it … It's my only regret," he says.

Making feature documentaries presented surprising challenges. "Perhaps it was also that it was such a jump from the commercial production environment I was used to shooting in for years—with total control and a feature crew—that I didn't know how to shoot at such a small level. So I just let it happen without injecting my visual sensibilities. I've since learned how to use visual language with a tiny crew in the service of a documentary," Aronson says.

Also perhaps to be filed under "Lessons Learned" … Even after Aronson met the Artinians and realized they were a perfect solution to his casting challenges, it didn't necessarily translate into smooth sailing the rest of the way. He had already shot a number of other people with fascinating angles on deafness to share and would continue to shoot others outside the Artinian family. He was toying with ways to weave them in with the Artinians and wasn't right away ready to give up on these people or this approach.

But trusted voices, including his girlfriend, tried to help him get over his multiple casting crushes, and to shun all but the Artinians. "It's hard to give up your babies, and I had really good babies. And I had to throw them all out. That was really hard," he says ruefully. But in the end, he had to admit it was the right and only move. "We ended up with the simplest possible structure with this family, and that is where the heart of the film was."

Through the Artinians alone, viewers get to mull over the weighty questions that drape the film, including: is deafness a kind of disability or a chosen lifestyle? Is it an illness that needs fixing, or is it a proactive and self-contained culture that needs no meddling from the hearing world? To Josh Aronson, who learned Sign Language to help make the film, it speaks to even broader concepts of assimilation that are familiar to marginalized groups everywhere. "I wanted this microcosm of the conflict in the deaf world to be seen as a metaphor for any minority group, asking 'Do you want to stay in, or do you want to stay out?'" During production, countless deaf people made sure Aronson got the message: "I'm not handicapped. I'm not disabled. I just can't hear. I'm part of the diversity of nature," as Aronson paraphrases.

Aronson's debut documentary not only stirred some of his own social views, Sound and Fury made its way into the popular culture as well. It played at Sundance, to great acclaim, followed by a wide festival tour. They nearly signed a distribution deal with a company they liked and which they met after Sundance. But a lucky case of cold feet held them back at the last minute, just before the company suddenly went out of business. They ended up signing a deal with Artistic License Films, who rolled out the film to theaters across the country and made it Oscar-eligible. An Oscar nomination followed, as did even more festival interest and countless requests for screenings and events with deaf organizations. Outreach to the deaf community continues apace, and the duo are still signing distribution deals with educational markets and others, some of them for screening formats that didn't exist when the film was made. "It's been an amazing ride," as Weisberg sums it up.

The Oscar nomination also, as one would expect, gave a career boost to Aronson. It allowed him to make more documentaries about matters that really spoke to his head and his heart, notably about issues of identity. After Sound and Fury, he made three films about transgendered people for Showtime. "It was basically the same issues for them (as in Sound and Fury), Who am I? Big, emotional identity stuff. Those are the kinds of films I want to make."

But he couldn't wander too far away from the Artinians. He made *Sound and Fury: 6 Years Later*, with dramatic updates all around. In the follow-up film, Heather, now 12 years old, her mother and 2 deaf siblings have all had the cochlear implants and seem to be adjusting well.

And in a fitting full-circle for a film blessed with so much serendipity, Aronson even got to re-connect with the woman who accidentally launched the film five years earlier. In 2000, at a screening filled with both deaf and hearing people, Aronson was telling the story of the woman he met on the street who said "I've got cochlear implants," and thereby planted the seed in Aronsons' head. All of a sudden, while he was telling this story, a hand shot up from the audience. "Mr. Aronson, I'm that woman!" The whole crowd stood up and applauded her.

13

Into the Arms of Strangers: Stories of the Kindertransport

DIRECTOR

Mark Jonathan Harris

PRODUCER

Deborah Oppenheimer

Oscar Winner, Best Documentary Feature—2000

SUMMARY

Into the Arms of Strangers: Stories of the Kindertransport *explores the fascinating and brief moment in history leading up to World War II when Britain opened its doors to 10,000 unaccompanied children from Germany, Austria, and Czechoslovakia who were at risk from the Nazi regime. The film explores how the children handled the traumas of dislocation and the challenges of leaving their families behind to be taken in by strangers.*

Celebrated documentary filmmaker and professor Mark Jonathan Harris had, his whole life, wished he could have asked questions to his much-loved grandfather, Samuel. TV Producer Deborah Oppenheimer, too, had long wanted to ask her mother, Sylva, about her own wrenching past, but her mother couldn't bring herself to talk about it. For both Harris and Oppenheimer, the questions were similar: how do children survive profound trauma?

Their shared, long-simmering curiosity would bring them together to create the magisterial and haunting film, *Into The Arms of Strangers: Stories of the Kindertransport*. He directed, and she was Producer. Of course, deep questions never yield easy answers, and the film would, for filmmakers and viewers, both fill in some blanks and also unleash an array of even more unanswerable questions. How children cope with acute upheaval is the narrative engine that drives on this quietly shattering film. *Kindertransport* explores the short-lived exodus of children from central Europe who left their families and escaped to Britain in the nine months just before the continent would erupt into World War II. Together, the 16 characters portrayed form a kind of memory collage, enlightening viewers, and easing the psychic hurts carried by the filmmakers as well.

Getting the film off the ground, though, took some work. By the late 1990s, Harris had been trying to look beyond Holocaust-related films. He'd directed the Oscar-winning *The Long Way Home* (1997), about Jewish refugees in the years just after World War II. He followed this highly successful film with a documentary about Israel, but its findings didn't jibe with those of the film's funders and it was never released. He was proud of this pair of films, but he also felt ready to explore new material. "I'd made a Holocaust film, and then a film on Israel, and I didn't want to make another. I didn't think I'd have anything more to say about these particular subjects," Harris recalls feeling at the time.

Around the same time, TV producer Deborah Oppenheimer, was actively researching the life of her mother, Sylva Avramovici, who had escaped Chemnitz, Germany, in 1939 at the age of 11. Sylva's parents put her on a London-bound train as part of the Kindertransport. Avramovici had died a few years earlier, and during her lifetime, she'd barely been able to share anything with Oppenheimer or her two siblings about her experiences with the

Kindertransport. The memories were simply too painful. "She'd start to talk, but then she'd just begin to cry," recalls Oppenheimer. Adds Harris: "There's a kind of passive agreement among the children that this is too painful to discuss so they never talk about it, and Deborah feels she never really understood her mother's story. There was always a kind of sadness in her mother, and they never got past that."

As Oppenheimer dug deeper into the Kindertransport, she was haunted and fascinated by what she was finding out. She was surprised to see there was a scarcity of material about this little-explored rescue effort, and she decided she needed to do what she could to fill in those gaps. A full-fledged documentary about these events, she realized, would have to be made.

She had the opportunity to speak with the head of HBO's renowned Documentary Unit, Sheila Nevins, to talk about the idea. To her surprise, Nevins offered to provide some initial development funds to help get it off the ground. But Oppenheimer was a producer of TV series' with no real documentary experience. She needed a high-caliber director to realize her vision with her, and she focused her attentions on Mark Harris.

"I had seen 'The Long Way Home' and thought it was wonderful. I thought Mark would be perfect for the film," says Oppenheimer. But when she approached Harris, his first response was a clear No. So she plied him with books and articles on the Kindertransport and tried to get him to see that their film would not be just another in the very long list of Holocaust movies. "I just didn't accept his rejection. I ignored it," says Oppenheimer. For his part, Harris recalls, "gradually she persuaded me. I began to see that it's really such a universal story. It's a story about separation of children from their parents. It's set in the backdrop of the Holocaust, but it's about the worst trauma a child could have, which is loss of parents and loss of home. And when I saw it in that way, I saw a way in which I could do it."

As with Oppenheimer, the story also had a deep personal resonance for Harris. The legend of Harris's grandfather, Samuel, loomed large in his family.

Samuel had fled anti-Jewish pogroms in late nineteenth-century Hungary at the age of 12, alone, and somehow managed to build a life for himself in America. But Samuel had died when Harris was just six, and Harris had always wondered how he managed to build his life from scratch, not conversant in English, and with almost no relatives around for support. "I was very close to [Samuel] as a child. He lived a block away from me and I saw him almost daily. Sadly … most of what I know about his history has come to me second hand," Harris wrote in an essay called "Breaking The Cycle."

United in their quest for answers, the film was both a professional pursuit and a personal one as well. The energy from each would provide fuel and curiosity to the other. Harris calls it, above all, "an exploration." And for him, there was yet another very personal layer to the story of the Kindertransport. He'd long been, on the side of his documentary and teaching careers, a writer of children's novels. He'd written several books aimed at a 12–13-year-old audience which focused on coping with problems in the adult world around them—such as divorce and homelessness. Like the war drumbeats swirling around children in late 1930s Europe, Harris notes that his books examined, albeit on a smaller scale, "problems children didn't cause but whose consequences they have to live with." *The Long Way Home* too explored how people of all ages try to re-build their lives after catastrophe. "Can you recover from it? That's a question I'm deeply interested in."

Right away, the duo faced the daunting challenge of finding characters. With so many thousands of children and foster families having been a part of the Kindertransport, how was one to find and choose just a handful for the film?

Oppenheimer, Harris, and a team of researchers read everything they could about the topic, looked at tapes from the vast Shoah Foundation archives and other sources, and worked the phones relentlessly. The United States Holocaust Memorial Museum gave invaluable help too and would eventually became an official collaborator on the film. Over a couple of years starting in 1998, Harris estimates that they made contact with about 300 people.

"We wanted to get a real cross section," Harris explains. "We wanted people who represented a wide range of experiences. We wanted to understand how different people responded to the same basic trauma...I was looking for characters who are still struggling with the issue in some way because that creates some tension." He and Oppenheimer were acutely aware that the public was already exposed to vast amounts of material about the Holocaust. "What can we bring that's new to this story?" was a constant refrain, recalls Harris. "We wanted to try to get as close to the emotional core as possible, and as freshly as possible."

The search for characters was daunting. The Kindertransport sent children from several countries—including Germany, and German-occupied Austria and Czechoslovakia, to the United Kingdom. While many remained in the United Kingdom, others re-settled across the globe, and yet others had died. There were very few parents who had put their children on the trains and survived to be reunited with them, and less than a handful of surviving rescuers.

Kindertransport organizers had hoped that the United States and other countries would also accept unaccompanied children fleeing Europe, but they were rebuffed. In the US House of Representatives, a bill supporting US participation died in Committee. Only the United Kingdom agreed to do so. A number of relief groups there and in the United States had monitored the Kindertransport since its inception and helped the filmmakers with referrals and introductions.

At the end of the day, Harris and Oppenheimer would simply have to interview a massive amount of people, many of them with amazing stories to tell, and then trust their gut instincts and make tough decisions about who would be included in the film. They set out to find about 20 people to interview on camera, and the plan was to screen all the interviews after that. If they felt that was too many characters to reasonably fit into the film, they'd have to then make some painful choices before editing. But they were so inundated with powerful material that they decided to put out a companion book with the film that would contain some of the stories that didn't make it.

After they'd gotten deeper into their search for characters and had filmed two time-sensitive interviews with ailing survivors, they brought a treatment and some footage and tried—unsuccessfully—to secure more funding from HBO.

Without the funds to move forward, Oppenheimer, a TV producer with a long track record, came up with a back-up plan. She'd produced some TV shows under contract with Warner Brothers, including hits like The Drew Carey Show. She asked executives there to fund her documentary, and they agreed, fearing that the survivors were getting on in years and that the stories could be lost. Not only did they agree to fund it, they also agreed "to leave us alone ... there were no corporate executives around," Harris notes with a smile.

They'd tapped out the initial HBO funds, but that money had allowed them to interview the indelible character Norbert Wollheim, whose testimony in the film is riveting. Wollheim was one of the few surviving rescuers, on an epic scale, and Harris and Oppenheimer were very eager to speak with him. He saved about 6,000 children during the War, but eventually he, his wife and child were deported to Auschwitz. At the selection, his wife and child were sent in one direction and he in another. He never saw them again. He suffered the cruel irony of having saved so many children but ultimately proving unable to save his own. Five weeks after sharing this story for the film, Wollheim died. His wife later told the filmmakers she believed he'd saved himself for one last testimony, for Harris and Oppenheimer's camera.

Since the scope of the film was so wide, the casting trail was, not unexpectedly, littered with surprises. They were very keen, for example, to interview a particular Kindertransport survivor still living in England. They'd read her memoir and were convinced she'd be perfect. So they sent a location manager to her house to make sure the space was suitable. The manager called them from the United Kingdom to discuss the location and mentioned that the woman's sister was in town at the time too, by chance, and would be worth speaking with as well. They went to the house, interviewed both sisters but felt the first sister's testimony lacked urgency and felt a little canned since she'd told it by then in a book and on many other occasions. "People aren't actors. And it's hard for most people to tell stories better the second time. Her sister hadn't really spoken to people very much before… she was fantastic." They opted to use her visiting sister's story in the film, and she would end up being one of the film's most compelling characters.

One interviewee told the film crew that she'd been haunted for years by nightmares since her childhood. "The interview was much more emotional for her than she expected. Then afterwards she told us that after giving this interview, her nightmares stopped. I think there can be a therapeutic quality in this, talking to a sympathetic stranger about this," says Harris. Harris' cinematographer, veteran shooter Don Lenzer, told him he'd never shot so many interviews with tears in his eyes. "I just got so swept up in the intensity of these characters. These were some of the most emotional interviews I'd ever done," recalls Harris.

Harris had honed his interview techniques not just in his documentary films over the years but going back even further to his days as a young crime reporter in Chicago. "We talked about issues they'd been struggling with for years, and the memories and revisiting them was just very emotional for many people. For all of us it was a privilege to actually hear these stories." Oppenheimer's involvement, as the child of a Kindertransport survivor, was also critical in helping to open up interviewees who may not have otherwise been so revealing. "It gave me a kind of credibility," she acknowledges.

Sometimes, it would take high doses of old-fashioned patience and persistence to do the trick. Harris was interviewing the adoptive mother of one of the Kindertransport survivors, and she told him she didn't want to talk

about a pivotal concept—how hard it was to give up her son after his birth
parents returned for him after the War. "I was thinking, 'I've just come 6,000
miles from California.' I was going to just sit there until she talked. So I let
that question pass and then came back to it again and again. By the third time,
finally she was willing to reveal how difficult that was."

Surprising patterns emerged as well. One point in particular stuck out to
Harris. He noticed that almost every single Kindertransport survivor they
interviewed related the same coda to their journey from the continent to
England. Almost all believed that they were the very last to be picked up at the
train station up by their adoptive families. "This couldn't actually have been
the case for all of them, but it's fascinating how many people believed this."

Harris and Oppenheimer realized that their quest for answers about
childhood trauma was pushing them into emotional territory beyond what
they'd even reckoned. The famous British "stiff upper lip" melted away for
many of the characters once they got deeper into telling their stories. And they
were consistently amazed by how many of the survivors told them they were
relating parts of their journey they'd never shared before, even with family
members.

"When I approach an interview, I try to listen to not just the words, but
also to the music. You try to respond to the underlying feelings, to feel out the
subtext and try to draw it out," says Harris of his methods for coaxing difficult
emotions. "I don't do the 'What happened? What happened next?' approach. I
try to respond to what I'm feeling, and what the subject is feeling."

And for Oppenheimer, making the film was itself a way to help lift the veil
that had shrouded much of her mother's Kindertransport experiences. "I saw
the film as a tribute to my mother. I could never have made this film if my
mother was alive," she says. While working on the film, in addition to revelations
about the broader Kindertransport, she discovered lots of details about her
mother's plight, about her foster family, and stories about her mostly unhappy
life in a succession of placements in the United Kingdom during the War.

Though her mother inspired and figured abstractly in the film, the irony was that she could not be in the film. Intimates of Sylva Avramovici can still catch glimpses of her—in some still shots, her parents' words in some of the letters read aloud and in some of the objects of her German childhood that make up the film's ravishing opening sequence.

Authenticity was paramount for the filmmakers; so, the various toys and books in those opening shots are all actual effects brought to the United Kingdom on the Kindertransport provided to the filmmakers from survivors. Likewise for the music—not reproductions but the actual recordings of music that would have been heard by Kindertransport children at that time.

In Post-Production, Harris and his editor, veteran talent Kate Amend, looked hard for ways to give a fresh vantage point to the archival material they'd need for context. One device they used was to actively search for material that showed how the Nazi era looked from the child's point of view. "This allowed us to find some footage that others had overlooked, like shots of Nazi guards' boots, as seen from a child's height, or a balloon floating away."

It was likewise with sound. The film's multiple Oscar-winning sound designer Gary Rydstrom threw out the playbook. "Gary saw this as a film about memories. And memory sounds are often very indistinct, except for every once in a while when something is extremely vivid. So he said, 'I don't want any clichés. I want to create all of the sounds except for the trains, and I don't want to use any sounds of boots marching.'" So they muted whatever ambient sound there was attached to the archive and created an entire tone-based soundscape. It helps lift the material by taking viewers into a kind of free-floating audio space, underscoring the unusual take on the familiar that they were aiming for.

They also aimed to bring a new angle to the Holocaust film. Oppenheimer said, "We wanted to ask of the audience the unanswerable questions—would you send your child away? Would you take in a child? We asked each of the survivors that question, but out of respect for the painful decision their parents made, they did not presume to know what they would really do in such unique circumstances."

They also worked to trim as much of the historical context as they possibly could, without leaving viewers confused. "We needed enough context for people to appreciate the stories, but we wanted this to be a dramatic film and not a history lesson," says Harris. "I think I always overwrite, and then cut back. With editing it's just like that."

They edited over 1999 and 2000 and premiered at the Toronto International Film Festival that Fall. A theatrical release across the United States followed, with enthusiastic support from Warner Bros. The Oscar win followed, and the filmmakers have been very busy ever since. Fifteen years after *Into The Arms Of Strangers*, the film's basic questions still haunt Harris. His newest project is about a professional hockey player who was sexually abused by a coach. "After that kind of trauma, how do you fix your life?" he asks.

For almost all involved, making "Kindertransport" was a harrowing, charged ordeal like almost no other. Harris recalls walking into the edit room at one point to screen a scene that editor Kate Amend had just cut. After watching the scene, Harris's eyes are swollen with tears. Said Amend: "I guess those are your notes."

CONVERSATION POINTS

Chapter 1: *Food, Inc.*

- This topic has been taken on by other journalists and documentarians, but big corporations and legal teams made it excruciating for them to proceed. Why and how did these filmmakers succeed?
- What steps should documentary filmmakers take to protect themselves legally when they are challenging deep-pocketed companies or individuals?
- When facing constant rejection of interview requests up and down the corporate "food chain," at what point should filmmakers simply decide that it is not possible to continue with a subject?

Chapter 2: *Man on Wire*

- The film's main subject had a sizable ego and was notoriously difficult to manage. What are some of the best techniques learned by how the *Man on Wire* team handled their tricky subject?
- The film had very large strong stretches with dramatized footage. Was it effectively used? What are the risks of using dramatization to tell a documentary?
- The film's subject strung the producer and director along in many ways before he agreed to even participate in the film. Are there techniques the filmmakers deployed to "snag" him that could be applied to other non-fiction subjects?

Chapter 3: *Super Size Me*

- Morgan Spurlock's crew put in many hours working for the film without any compensation. Much of it was deferred. As a director, how do you persuade partners to make these kinds of sacrifices for you and your vision?
- After casting around for someone to act as an on camera guide for his story, Spurlock gave up and decided to cast himself. Was this a risky move? Was it the wise move?

– Spurlock subjected himself to repeat on camera embarrassing moments and situations. Did these take away from the overall serious subject matter of the film, or enhance it?

Chapter 4: *Twenty Feet from Stardom*

– What kinds of techniques for clearing music rights can we learn from a master like Morgan Neville?
– What does it mean for filmmakers when private investors fund a film? What are their most appropriate roles, if any, in the production?
– Morgan Neville kept trying to find his exact story, even during Post. Is this a risky approach or wise?
– Simple advice for persuasion: when asking for a favor, take the person to lunch. It's hard to say no over lunch.

Chapter 5: *Spellbound*

– The filmmakers had a massive group of kids that could have gone on to win the spelling bee. But they could only follow a small number, given time and budget. How did they decide who to follow?
– At a spelling bee, much of the drama goes on "backstage," among family members and contestants. How did the filmmakers weave in both backstage and onstage elements?
– The director racked up massive credit card debt to make this film. Besides the obvious financial risks of debt, what impact does this method of funding have on production?

Chapter 6: *The Act of Killing*

– The filmmaker had to take enormous precautions to stay safe in the charged environment he worked in for so long. How did he work to stay safe?
– The director was working with horrific subject matter. How can a filmmaker stay mentally focused in spite of spirit-crushing material?
– The director interviewed several dozen former killers but ended up focusing the film mostly on just one of them. Is that because this person represents the rest or does it become a more anecdotal look at one man?

Chapter 7: *GasLand*

- Directors and filmmakers come from all walks of life. How does a director from a theater background—used to fictionalizing his work—apply his skills to a non-fiction story?
- If you're clever enough, you don't always need money or a studio to get the priceless opinions of a focus group. What are some other ways to gather this information?
- What are the potential benefits and potential drawbacks of putting yourself front and center in your film?

Chapter 8: *Undefeated*

- While creating their documentary, a major Hollywood narrative film was made and released about similar subject matter. The documentary filmmakers choose to basically ignore it. Is it necessary to do so to stay focused?
- The two main filmmakers edited the film together in a vibrant, high pressure atmosphere. What are the risks of teaming up in this way?
- The filmmakers moved across the country to live among the subjects of their film. What are the benefits of doing this? Are there any downsides to this kind of immersive filmmaking?

Chapter 9: *Restrepo*

- The director went to dangerous lengths to gather the material in this film, embedded with soldiers in a notoriously hostile area. Is this the best, or even the only, way to gather these kinds of images and tell these kinds of stories?
- Journalist turned documentarian Junger was sent to Afghanistan for a print article—but with lucid foresight, he brought a camera. How can one juggle the sometimes conflicting needs of both print and documentary?

Chapter 10: *Sergio*

- The director took the very bold step of dramatizing a nightmarish and pivotal scene. Are the scenes done effectively and what steps does he take to keep those scenes from looking cheesy or maudlin?

- Many of the main character's friends and colleagues are very reluctant to say anything on camera that could seem critical about him. Is it the director's job to draw them out or simply to work within those limitations?
- How did the filmmaker make the transition from hard news to long form documentary? What are the challenges people face when they make this transition?

Chapter 11: *Maya Lin: A Strong Clear Vision*

- The director kept this fascinating story in the back of her mind until the time was right to make a film about it. What's the best way to "tend to" an idea, even for years, until you're able to make it a film?
- The subject of the film was reluctant to allow the director to focus on her personally. Is it up to the director to push for personal access or is it better to defer to your subject on this matter?
- The director had to fundraise almost all the way through production—not an uncommon scenario. How can a person stay focused on the story line and produce in the face of financial worries?

Chapter 12: *Sound and Fury*

- What are the special technical and ethical challenges posed by working with the deaf?
- Will viewers forgive aesthetically unpleasing footage when they're captivated by the story?
- What are the difficulties faced when making the move from commercials and industrials straight into feature-length theatrical documentaries?
- Josh Aronson took a random conversation on the street and turned it into inspiration and a film. Is this a good way to launch a film?

Chapter 13: *Into the Arms of Strangers: Stories of the Kindertransport*

- It's difficult, but usually vital and helpful, to cut back on interviewees—even ones the filmmakers love. How to decide who stays in the film?
- The director and, particularly, the producer had strong personal motivations guiding their production. Is this necessary in order to create powerful films?
- The filmmakers took great pains to reveal new angles and new story-telling techniques on sometimes familiar material. Why is this important?

SOURCES

1. Interview with Morgan Spurlock, May 21, 2013
2. Interview with Sebastian Junger, March 3, 2014
3. Interview with T.J. Martin, July 2, 2012
4. Interview with Daniel Lindsay, October 3, 2012
5. Interview with Josh Aronson, November 7, 2013
6. Interview with Roger Weisberg, March 18, 2014
7. Interview with Robert Kenner, March 23, 2012
8. Interview with Elise Pearlstein, March 2, 2012
9. Interview with Greg Barker, March 21, 2014
10. Interview with Simon Chinn, March 22, 2012
11. Interview with James Marsh, March 18, 2014
12. Interview with Jeffrey Blitz, June 6, 2012
13. Interview with Mark Harris, February 24, 2012
14. Interview with Deborah Oppenheimer, June 1, 2014
15. Interview with Morgan Neville, May 15, 2014
16. Interview with Joshua Oppenheimer, May 9, 2014
17. Interview with Frieda Lee Mock, June 2, 2014
18. Interview with Josh Fox, April 2, 2014

INDEX